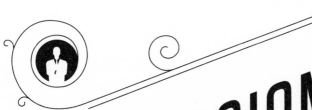

PROFESSIONAL
PRESENCE

A Four-Part Guide *to* Building
Your Personal Brand

PEGGY NOE STEVENS

GREENLEAF
BOOK GROUP PRESS

Published by Greenleaf Book Group Press
Austin, Texas
www.gbgpress.com

Distributed by Greenleaf Book Group LLC

For ordering information or special discounts for bulk purchases,
please contact Greenleaf Book Group LLC at PO Box 91869, Austin,
TX 78709, 512.891.6100.

Design and composition by Greenleaf Book Group LLC
Cover design by Greenleaf Book Group LLC
Illustrations by Phil Wilson

Publisher's Cataloging-In-Publication Data
(Prepared by The Donohue Group, Inc.)
Stevens, Peggy Noe.
    Professional presence : a four-part guide to building your personal
brand / Peggy Noe Stevens. — 1st ed.
      p. : ill. ; cm.
    Includes bibliographical references.
    ISBN: 978-1-60832-279-4
    1. Success in business. 2. Self-actualization (Psychology) 3.
Branding (Marketing) 4. Business etiquette. 5. Charisma (Personality
trait) I. Title.
HF5386 .S74 2012
650.13   2011941852

Part of the Tree Neutral® program, which offsets the number of
trees consumed in the production and printing of this book by taking
proactive steps, such as planting trees in direct proportion to the
number of trees used: www.treeneutral.com

Printed in the United States of America on acid-free paper

11 12 13 14 15 16   10 9 8 7 6 5 4 3 2 1

First Edition

To my father, the ultimate diplomat who exemplified Professional Presence.

CONTENTS

INTRODUCTION
CREATING YOUR PERSONAL BRAND

What is your brand?

When I talk to audiences across the United States, it never fails to amaze me how quickly they respond when I show slides of famous brands: Coke, Nike, Disney. The audience members shout out descriptors, showing that they are intimately familiar with the brand and its message. As soon as I say the brand *Nike,* a melodic *swoosh* sound seems to come from the audience. *Coke* immediately brings *the color red, refreshing, Americana.* It is incredibly easy for the audience to recognize brand essence and physical attributes of top brands.

Then I challenge the audience to identify the next brand, the brand that is most important for their personal success. I pause for a moment before putting up a slide with one word: *you.*

The silence is stunning. Blank faces stare back at me.

This amazes me too. The audience knows the iconic brands, but people have nothing to say about their own brand.

I immediately jump in to encourage them. "Tell me what the brand *you* says? How do people describe you? What is your icon? What is your trademark? What experience do you represent?"

After a very long pause, people normally pick up their pens and press them to paper, still waiting for the image to come to their minds. It is surprising to me still. After all, *this is your brand*. The brand that no one should know better than you do.

Brands today don't just happen. Virtually thousands of images large and small inform us about brands over time. Marketers take painstaking care when creating a brand's persona, and when linking that persona to the brand's image. I think of iconic brands such as Coke, Nike, and Disney, and immediately memories of their icons, colors, and slogans begin to play in my head. These images create subliminal connotations and impressions in my mind, encouraging me as a consumer to respond to the message either negatively or (the marketers hope) positively.

Whether I am a fan or not, every image of the brand calls to mind my experience with that brand. These experiences affect my attitude toward the branded product and the company behind the product. I form an opinion of the brand, which influences how I will relate to the brand in the future. The brand, in other words, makes an impression on me that affects my decisions regarding the product. Does the brand attract me to the product, or does it send me looking for something else? Does the brand inspire me to invest in the product, or does it cause me to spend my time and money elsewhere?

Your personal brand has the same impact on those around you. The various impressions you make on other individuals influence their reaction to you, and this can have a profound influence on your personal and professional life. You would never intentionally create a brand for yourself that made a negative impression on others. But too often individuals do exactly that, when they are unaware of the message, look, feel, and voice of the brand they are building. To create a positive impression that leads to success, you need to create a strong personal brand with a solid story and valuable content. *Professional Presence* will help you do just that.

So, what is your brand exactly? Your brand is your image. To manage your brand, you must manage your image. And to manage your image, you must first learn the basics of building and maintaining an image.

Others form impressions of you with every encounter. Each word you speak or gesture you make delivers an impression, good or bad. No matter where you are in your career life cycle, you have (or you are in the midst of forming) a brand that will be the foundation for your success or failure. How solid is that foundation?

People seem to refer to the all-important resume as their personal brand. Granted, the resume does describe your past accomplishments, business experience, and so forth, which is a good indication of your brand framework. Some resumes are quite impressive in this way, with scads of credentials and title marks. If you believe that your personal brand is constructed solely by these words on a single sheet of paper, however, you are wrong. Your way of speaking, your methods of social interaction, and your appearance are equally important parts of your personal brand. This is the reason companies don't hire employees based solely on their resumes.

We all walk into jobs with our particular credentials—degrees, designations, affiliations. But there is no certificate in professional presence—no established professional code of conduct—and there should be. Companies interview in an attempt to diagnose early on whether the candidate will be a good "fit" for the company—that is, will your personal brand fit the company's brand? And when it is time for a promotion, companies look not only at a candidate's success record but also at the person as a whole: Can you grow within the company and aspire to be a future leader? The answers to these questions are based on your brand.

In short, while much of your personal brand is based on your education, experience, and technical skills, your brand is very much shaped and defined by your social skills.

The social skills discussed in this book are absolutely indispensible to your brand, your image, and your career. You may be rewarded and recognized at times for your hard work and accomplishments, but your career will not advance unless you master these social skills, polish your image, and define your personal brand.

I traveled an unexpected career path to reach where I am today. The journey was not without failures, adjustments, and hard work. No one provided me with a "career GPS" to lead me to the levels that I have now achieved. Few people were available to show me the right and wrong turns ahead. Like everyone, I found myself learning from my mistakes.

I tested many techniques of brand building, particularly during my work experience at a major corporation. I received some bumps and bruises along the rocky corporate path, but they helped me figure out the importance of these techniques and benefit from them. Once you have mastered my lessons, they will help you meet some of the challenges of building your personal brand.

My experience has led me to many conclusions about what makes the "whole employee" and about the importance of developing a personal brand for career advancement. I have spent many years watching employees strive to develop their careers. I have worked extensively with human resource managers to help train and educate employees. I have collaborated with dozens of senior executives and CEOs, and I can tell you what human resources can't.

Companies are very effective in teaching individuals how to improve their technical skills, but many times they are deficient when it comes to showing employees how to develop their personal brand. This is because most managers themselves are not aware of what it takes to build a personal brand. Most individuals don't consciously set out to create their brand. If they are lucky, they have personal traits that add luster to their brand. The unlucky ones, however, never develop a strong brand—or worse, they develop a brand that hurts their career. Learning to create and enhance your brand can truly become a discipline. Feedback, self-awareness, and willingness to change are key to crafting a strong brand, and doing so without losing your authenticity is a real balancing act.

Creating a personal brand may seem overwhelming at first. That is why, over the years, I have developed a simple process that will enable you to build your brand one step at a time. My firm helps people and organizations use this process to build a professional brand, and this book shares the skills and techniques involved. The book will take you through the process and allow you to create a personal brand that will be the foundation for your career success.

The branding process is organized around four "professional presence platforms": Protocol, Personal, Professional, and People. Each platform—covered in parts I through IV of this book—introduces essential skills for developing your brand. Each of these fourteen skills examines areas of concentration and focus that will allow you to assess your individual strengths and weaknesses. You will be able to break down and analyze your personal brand in regard to each aspect of the platforms—and then use the action-oriented skills to build a brand that extends far beyond your resume.

Building your brand means learning how to deal with a variety of business situations, including presenting at a board meeting, staging a power lunch, and dealing with dress-code disasters. If you lack these skills, if you are tentative in public, and if you are prone to making mistakes when you step out of your office and lead in person, you will not project a strong brand. You will miss opportunities and you will get passed over. I have watched too many rising stars begin their ascension to the top of the ladder only to topple before making it to the upper rungs because they fail to convey and exude a professional image. You can stand in the way of your own success because of the ways you were taught, or the ways you learned on your own, the softer side of business.

I understand that men and women bring different perspectives to their experience in the workplace. While generalizations aren't always constructive, we know from management and social science research that gender and background affect how we see ourselves and others. The way you are *perceived* affects the reality of your life. When you ignore or deny this reality, you're simply choosing to undermine your own goals. People matter—and being a man or a woman is a big part of who we are as people! This book will give you insights to understand the strengths and weaknesses of our roles as men and women in America. You will learn how to align your body language, speech, and style to accentuate your strengths and minimize your weaknesses. This is a key part of building your personal brand.

In developing this book, I have kept in mind the stress we all experience while balancing work, family, and other responsibilities. The chapters are short and to the point. The skills and exercises will allow you to accomplish a great deal in a minimal amount of time. Mastery will come from repetition and practice. You can visit my website and blog at www.peggynoestevens.com to learn more, read corporate case studies, get tips, and hear interviews with leaders.

Whatever your role in a company, with this book you'll learn how to do more and achieve more—without losing yourself. You'll learn how to gain responsibility and use authority. You'll learn how to lead from your strengths, and you'll discover that the only "big picture" in your company is you. Employees can become lost in large corporations, never knowing which way to turn to improve their careers. This book places you in the driver's seat with a panoramic view, by improving your skills and enabling you to interact with your colleagues and engage in the corporate environment.

The behaviorist Charles Helliwell wrote the following in 2008 (in "Challenging Workplace Conventions," www.bpaudits.co.uk):

We all rely on someone else, or something else, to define our working lives: what jobs we do and how our employers, colleagues, customers, and the world at large see us. As children, it is our parents, immediate family, and schooling. As adults, it is our family, our friends, our colleagues, our employers, our religions, and our wealth, to name but a few. A new job or a change of career is determined by another person's assessment of a curriculum vitae or resume, which may bear little, if any, reflection of an individual's working day.

By learning the professional presence, we rely on ourselves more than on any of these outside influences. We take charge of our brand and our identity. We make choices based on long-established precedent and practice. This gives us the confidence to express our personality in work and service, which allows us to succeed.

The irony you will soon discover is this: By being true to your own brand, you will stop worrying about pleasing others so much, while actually gaining more respect and authority. You will begin to act and decide with confidence and authenticity. Your brand and your image will develop naturally and will propel you to career success.

So many employees wait to be tapped on the shoulder for promotion, or they think that the HR department is well versed in their personal brand and will seek them out, only to find themselves stalled in their careers. It's time for you to take charge. Learn the techniques of professional presence, and you can build the personal brand that will take you to the top.

PART I: PROTOCOL

I don't care what all the books say—the best form of

etiquette is to make people feel comfortable.

OVERVIEW

What is *protocol*?

Many people mock protocol, usually because they do not understand what it is and why it's important. Others give protocol a bad rap because they believe it connotes stiffness, refinement, or an uneasy, rule-bearing mentality.

Business protocol is quite truly the opposite of these things. At its base, it is nothing more than a set of guidelines for behavior in social and business settings. It can bring civility to the workplace, project a comfortable decorum during interactions with others, and offer a road map for relationship building.

When working with individuals or giving speeches, I describe protocol as the understanding that creates a distraction-free environment. As I see it, we are all walking the same path and trying as hard as we can to respect our mutual human wants and needs. As we walk the path together, we want it to be distraction free—free of obstacles that could hinder our ability to communicate with and understand one another. How can we expect individuals to appreciate our personal brand if they are distracted by billboards and e-mail? It's like looking at a package with too many labels: It speaks loudly and stands out, but not in an appealing way. When you finally open the product, you will discover whether you like it or not. Did the product deliver on the promise of the external package? Did it fall short? Or did it pleasantly surprise you by being even more fabulous than the package represented? The act of removing distractions is a key component of our personal brand.

Professional presence is thinking before acting, taking into account what is the right thing to do. It is thinking about how I can act in a way that will make others feel at ease. It is considering things as complicated as how I relate to my boss during a crisis or as simple as how I introduce myself to someone and follow up later. Making the effort to act appropriately allows others to feel comfortable in our presence and makes us feel comfortable in theirs. Who doesn't want this in their life? And in this composed, distraction-free environment, created by the simple act of following protocol, you can effectively display your brand.

I like to refine the concept of *protocol* by placing the word *human* before it, because I feel strongly that we have lost so much of what is "human" in our workplace, yet that defines our personal brand like nothing else. People are motivated by many things in business—money and title foremost among them—but at the end of the day, we all need to be valued in the workplace and to feel that we are contributing and being appreciated. It is the human side of the coin that I focus on here, because if you understand your business environment from a professional presence perspective, you will achieve far greater respect from others. In the course of my career, I assure you, there were many times that I fell off the protocol wagon because my emotions misguided me or I created needless distractions in situations where I was uncomfortable. I hope to prevent you from doing the same thing.

This section will teach you the proper protocol for engagement in social situations and day-to-day business. We will discuss the essentials of poise and etiquette and their effects in the workplace and business social settings. As you read this chapter, you will learn to master the following skills:

- **Skill #1:** Discovering the Power of Poise
- **Skill #2:** Mastering Business Etiquette
- **Skill #3:** Developing Touchpoint Etiquette

SKILL #1
DISCOVERING THE POWER OF POISE

Knowing the difference between *pose* and *poise* is crucial. Many professionals put on various faces at work, striking the poses they hope will impress team members and superiors. There's a problem with posing, though. Sometimes, when you encounter a challenging situation, you forget to pose. Then where are you? You are faking it. Others pick up on that quickly. This can cause them to assume that your entire personal brand is fake.

Projecting a poised, reassuring image is easily learned but quickly lost. Poise, defined by Merriam-Webster as "an easy self-possessed assurance of manner," is the essence of putting individuals at ease when they are in your company. Poise comes from being authentic and comfortable with your own personality, and it is the foundation for all of the business social skills. My favorite example of the power of poise is the following: Say you are dealing with a certain person at work who interacts with you a certain way, and then a higher-level manager or executive enters the room. Suddenly the demeanor of your co-worker changes right before your eyes. You stare at her and wonder, *Who is this person? Why does he/ she relate to me one way when a superior is around, and another way when a superior is not around?*

Why do people pose with one group, then behave differently with another? The answer is simple: They believe they have something to gain by treating certain people with greater regard. Those who demonstrate *poise*, on the other hand, treat people at every level with the same degree of respect and honor.

Poise also depends on being comfortable with the culture that surrounds you. To add the power of poise to your personal brand, first and foremost you need to understand the current culture of your company. How poised are the executives and managers? In even the largest companies, there is seldom a written guideline about demonstrating poise or about other aspects of protocol. This can be confusing to employees, who are forced to guess about what guides company behavior. Yet every company establishes a culture, even if it is informal or unwritten. As you establish your personal brand, you don't want to become just a walking billboard for the company, but you certainly need to be mindful of the company culture. Navigating the culture in your own way while maintaining respect for "the way things are done" is the first step to developing poise.

Now let's dig into specifics by identifying techniques that will help you use the power of poise to build your brand in three important areas: conversation, confident gestures, and clothes.

THE THREE C'S OF POISE

1. Conversation

What do I say? This is usually the question I get from employees who feel awkward about conversing with someone else. Conversation and poise go hand in hand because your words become your actions. You speak not just with your mouth but with your entire body. By mastering visual listening and learning to read body language, you add to your level of poise, because you can either mirror the image a person is presenting or do the opposite to avoid a conflict.

In conversation, you have to rely on poise to create a distraction-free zone so the person you are talking with can focus on your message and appreciate your brand. You speak every day to certain people and in certain situations without any problem, but what triggers the moment when you are distracted—when you suddenly become short on words? At that moment when you become speechless, what has happened? Are you intimidated by authority, or embarrassed because you just don't know the answer? What triggered this moment of "blank"? Or what caused you to say just the wrong thing, forcing your conversation partner to disengage? Getting behind the problem to understand why we have "quiet panics" or "mind blanks" is crucial to performing optimally in any conversation.

Below are some techniques that will keep you from losing your poise during a difficult conversation.

Approach

It is important that you take time to understand the who, what, when, and where *before* you are engaged in conversation. People never seem to take enough time to think before acting. When following professional presence, you will build the framework for a conversation by taking the time to assess the environment you are walking into. This is key to preparing your approach in terms of your style of conversation, the temperament you choose, and the appropriate level of casualness or formality. Who is the person you are dealing with? What will be the subject of your conversation? Is this person going through a tough time, or has he/she just received a promotion? Is the person ego-driven, or quiet and shy? What type of messages will he/she respond to? Above all else, how can you make this person feel comfortable when you approach?

Voice

In our everyday speech, we rarely use our ability to dial our voices up or down. When I am training employees on voice, we read aloud from a book. I ask them to read as if they are an actor reciting from a script or a parent reading a bedtime story to his/her children. The purpose of this is for them to notice the rise and fall of their voices. We pinpoint where they choose to exaggerate words and where they use a quieter tone.

A lot can be inferred from how you articulate and the inflection you use when speaking. Your speech is more effective when you match the tone and cadence (or balance) of your voice with the desired impact; your message is much more powerful if your words are supported by your voice. People will listen more closely to you when you are not speaking in a monotone, too quietly, or louder than necessary. Being purposeful and methodic, and choosing words carefully to describe your message, shows a great amount of poise.

Conversely, listen to others' voices as they speak, and again you will get a "human read" on how they are feeling about the subject. Does the speaker have a shaky voice because he/she is nervous, or does his or her voice become louder when arguing a point? One technique in using your conversational skills to support your poise is learning to understand how others may emphasize a point, and, when possible, using that same vocal technique to emphasize your own points. When you use a tone that is familiar to the person you are speaking with, he or she will be more able to relate to what you are saying. This is not recommended all the time, of course, because the person's tone may not be one you wish to mirror—for example, if he or she is nervous. But it can help to support a conversation if, say, someone is very enthusiastic and excited about an opportunity, and your voice mirrors that excitement to support the communication.

Breathing

Another *very* important technique for speech is quite simple: Breathe! Speaking from your throat indicates a weakness of voice, which implies a weakness of your brand. Speak from the diaphragm instead to push air through evenly. I know a public speaker who spoke so much from his throat that he scarred his vocal cords. To save his voice, he had to relearn how to speak from his diaphragm. There is a bonus to this method: Breathing properly allows you to pause between sentences, which gives the appearance of control and fluidity.

Redirecting

This is a technique to use when conversations are off base, lose focus, or just get out of hand. Use your internal radar to recognize when redirecting is needed—that is, when the conversation veers off topic or emotion takes over. To regain control of the conversation, use phrases like "Thank you for making that point" or "I appreciate that feedback"—and then move on with your topic.

When someone keeps pushing to veer off on another subject, take a break. If you are at a social gathering, it might be a good time to move on to someone else. If you are in a meeting, a five-minute cooldown may be necessary. You can always pull the person aside and say that although you think his/her opinions are important, you need to stay on task. After an interruption, you may even ask respectfully to table that topic until the end of the meeting, and then you can circle back to it if time allows. When you do not know the answer to a particular question, try saying, "May I look into that and get back to you?" It is OK not to have all the answers in your back pocket. Rather than look like a fool, tap-dancing around a topic because you are not certain what to say about it, wait until you know the answer and can present it thoughtfully.

Emotion

Do you check your emotional status before you enter into a conversation? Are you steamed? Lethargic? Feeling good? Knowing your emotions will play a role in how effective you are in connecting with the other person. Have you ever left behind a bad conversation only to walk into another, still carrying the anger and then taking it out on an unassuming person? Starting a conversation with heated subliminal emotions threatens your connection with that unassuming person. Don't let a harried, stressed morning at home carry over into the first meeting at work by rushing in the door, looking unorganized and out of sorts. Your blameless colleagues don't deserve it and certainly will not appreciate the bad energy.

Connection

This is just another word for *engagement*. Are you getting through to the person? Is he/she engaged in the conversation and understanding your message? What is the person's reaction to what you are saying? If you are reading his or her body language, great—that is a surefire indication that you are connecting. If in doubt, however, why not ask? Ask if the person understands what you are trying to say and how he/she is feeling about the comments or information. I don't know about you, but my crystal ball sure gets fuzzy at times.

We rely too often on how we *think* the other person is reacting, and fail to register the reaction itself. Whether during a seminar or one-on-one training, I never hesitate to simply ask, "What do you think? How are you doing? Do you get it?" I've been blindsided many times when I walked out of a room *assuming* things were good, only to receive feedback later that someone did not like what I had to say or did not buy into the message. Make sure the connection is there—and ask if you have to.

Clarity

Your message must be clear, or there is no point to the conversation. A vital technique for putting the power of poise to use is to express your message in a positive manner. Even when your message is criticism, you need to connect clearly and positively with the individual, or you will lose him/her. When people are listening to an uncomfortable or negative message, they tune you out, turn inward, or spend their time thinking of a rebuttal or counterpoint to your message. Be clear that you want to hear what they have to say, but ask them to keep an open mind until you are finished, and assure them that they will gain a better understanding once they know the whole picture. Ending a negative conversation on a positive note is also helpful; tell the person what he/she is doing right, share some good news, or focus on achieving the ultimate goal.

 ## PRESENCE PRACTICE

To develop your conversation skills, think of three times when you were left speechless or when you stammered for the answer during a conversation. Write these down, and then take a step back for a moment. Was it the other person or the content of the conversation that made you feel uncomfortable? Look for themes in this area. Do these uncomfortable times stem from the other person's personality? From the message itself? Zero in on any particular challenges you face when it comes to conversation.

2. Confident Gestures

Effective gestures are the second aspect of the triumvirate that contributes to poise. Your gestures affect others, and you can learn to use the right ones to burnish your own brand. The purposeful and methodic flow of gestures can express your level of poise. Best of all, you will be pleasantly surprised at how easy it is to understand the language of gestures.

There are two basic kinds of gestures: open and closed. When your body language appears open—when you keep your body upright and your arms open—it symbolizes active listening and engagement. When your body position is closed and tight, with arms crossed, you are visually putting a gate up around yourself; the receiver will feel that you are guarded and not willing to listen. Posture is another indicator of closed and open communication. Never underestimate how much you can tell about someone by his or her poor posture. When someone rolls his or her shoulders or turns sideways in his or her chair, that person can also indicate that he/she is closed for business. When shoulders are back and the body is upright, this posture displays confidence and openness.

I always watch a presenter's posture because it helps me understand whether the person believes what he or she is saying and is proud of the message; if the speaker looks defeated, with hunched shoulders and a slumping spine, it leads me to believe that the message is less than genuine. Many gestures can have a dual meaning, depending on the situation and climate of interaction. As you become a connoisseur of nonverbal gestures, you will be able to tell which meaning the speaker is expressing.

Identified here are twenty-four common gestures that allow you to analyze speakers and listeners (that is, to get the "human read"):

1. Moving hand to mouth (deceit, or prevention of things that shouldn't be said)

2. Touching elbows (positive reassurance)

3. Rubbing neck (uncertainty)

4. Touching fingertips lightly (confidence)

5. Creating a steeple with fingertips (smugness or arrogance)

6. Touching body parts nervously or in agitation—for example, putting hair behind the ear, tugging on clothing, picking fingernails (insecurity)

7. Raising eyebrows (support or excitement)

8. Yawning (boredom or nervousness)

9. Furrowing brow (concentration or frustration)

10. Crossing arms (blocking people from entering your territory)

11. Leaving arms open and relaxed (active listening)

12. Clenching a coffee cup or pen (frustration, seeking comfort)

13. Tapping a foot or swinging a crossed leg (impatience)

14. Smirking (disbelief or sarcasm)

15. Pursing lips (listening and thinking, or hesitation about the message)

16. Clenching jaw (uptightness)

17. Chewing gum or mints quickly, or clenching jaw rapidly (agitation)

18. Moving arms in exaggeration (lack of control)

19. Placing one arm behind the back (looking for security)

20. Tilting head to one side or the other (inability to understand, or attempting to understand)

21. Using phone or BlackBerry while someone is speaking (disre-

spect, saying "you are not important")

22. Taking notes while someone is speaking (belief in the message's importance)

23. Sitting behind the desk while talking (claiming authority)

24. Sitting nearby while talking (encouraging connection)

This is just a quick rundown of nonverbal gestures that display a speaker's level of poise. You can use these gestures both to purposefully exhibit poise and to determine the level of poise exhibited by others. When your actions match your words and your intended message, your communication will be effective. But when there is a disconnect between your body language and your message, that message will not be believable.

 ## PRESENCE PRACTICE

Take thirty minutes to look in the mirror and demonstrate various gestures so you will see what others are seeing when you speak or listen to them. Ask your spouse or significant other, another family member, or a close personal friend whether you tend to use gestures that are duplicative and noticeable. Then demonstrate those images in the mirror again to see what he/she is seeing. Do you make facial expressions that can be misunderstood, like eye rolling or smirking? Pursed lips can be seen as disapproving, for example, and a furrowed brow could unintentionally suggest anger.

In time, you will develop the alertness and self-awareness needed to use nonverbal messaging effectively. It takes practice. I encourage people to make facial expressions in the mirror to see what others see. I once trained a young manager on facial expression because his boss and clients felt that he was sarcastic and overconfident, thanks to a crooked smile he used when he spoke. He was losing credibility and irritating his superiors and his peers, yet he did not realize he was doing this until he looked in the mirror and saw the smirk for himself. Once he became aware of this unintentional message and changed his facial expression, he received glowing reviews. Another young woman constantly sat sideways in her chair and tilted her head as she spoke. She lacked the confidence to look me straight on and physically show that she was open to the conversation. We worked on her positioning of her head and body, and a change was noticeable immediately. She became more confident and appeared as such to the people she encountered.

3. Clothing

Your physical presence is a critical factor in developing the power of poise. The key to that presence is what you wear. Essentially, clothing becomes a nonverbal gesture because it speaks of your brand, depending on the style you choose. You can't be poised if you feel uncomfortable with what you are wearing. Likewise, other people will not be able to relax around you if *they* feel uncomfortable with what you are wearing. My early mentors taught me that clothing is the most powerful nonverbal communication tool you have. The clothes you wear generate actual physical responses in those around you.

Clothing is much too important to discuss in detail here—so important, in fact, that it is discussed thoroughly as Skill #5. For now, just remember that clothes are essential to poise. When you look the part and strive to display your authentic style, it supports what you are trying to say about yourself. Think your wardrobe through; the nature of your audience also should dictate your choices. What you wear will determine how they perceive your level of professionalism, your approachability factor, and, believe it or not, your mood.

By developing poise through the three C's—conversation, confident gestures, and clothing—you will take a crucial step in developing your own personal brand. The way other people view you is much like taking a snapshot, when one looks through the camera lens and tries to fit everything into the image. There is no one thing that they focus on; it is the entire sensory image. Remember, your personal brand is dependent on that image . . . just as Nike depends on the swoosh.

 ## PRO SCENARIO: DISCOVERING THE POWER OF POISE

Jim, a copy machine salesperson, is meeting with Bob, a prospective client. Feeling confident, Jim arrives to the appointment right on time. He has showered, shaved, and picked out his best suit for the meeting. He knows his product, and he's ready for business.

Upon meeting his client, Jim introduces himself and shakes Bob's hand, looking him in the eye. Bob, however, isn't showing the same enthusiasm—he even seems to be annoyed. Jim explains his products to Bob, who sits slouched in his chair, arms crossed. Bob seems so disinterested that it causes Jim to get a bit nervous, and he ends up doing nearly all the talking. Concerned about wasting both his time and Bob's, Jim concludes the meeting shortly after it started.

Not long after his meeting with Jim, Bob purchases a copier . . . from Jim's competition.

Why didn't Bob purchase the equipment from Jim?

What did Jim do wrong?

What could Jim have done differently?

What lessons can you apply?

For my responses to these questions, visit my website, www.peggynoestevens.com.

SKILL #2
MASTERING BUSINESS ETIQUETTE

I was attending a business dinner party when a senior executive stopped by my seat and asked why so-and-so did not attend. I wasn't sure why that employee was absent (no RSVP had been made), but I told the executive that I would be happy to follow up with the individual.

The executive quickly replied, "No bother. I keep in mind the people whom I invite and who repeatedly do not show up or respond. They usually do not make my future guest list." If you think your absence will not be noticed, you are wrong. Being absent and failing to RSVP is often duly noted, and it leaves the host questioning the importance of your relationship.

Not many people will say they need etiquette training—but most people do need it. The terms *protocol* and *etiquette* are often used interchangeably; in this book, however, I refer to *protocol* as the guidelines for business interaction and to *etiquette* as the manners of business interaction. While most of us observe family and community etiquette (we don't wear a bathing suit to church, swear in front of our grandmother, or eat with our hands at Thanksgiving dinner), too many talented people in the business world forget the basics of business etiquette. Professionals also make mistakes by being unsure of how to introduce themselves, failing to pitch their skills, and neglecting the basic interactions of connecting.

"They don't teach etiquette much anymore," wrote Harvey Mackay, a great business advisor, "but if you ever have to choose between Incredibly Advanced Accounting for Overachievers and Remedial Knife and Fork, head for the silverware." Contemporary etiquette, contrary to popular belief, is not about channeling the British schoolmarm who stands in front of the class and taps your hand with a ruler when you don't use the right fork. Contemporary etiquette means knowing how to create a distraction-free environment so everyone is moving in the same respectful direction.

Using proper etiquette is vital to developing your personal brand, so it is necessary that you understand and observe the essential techniques of business etiquette in key situations.

THE ESSENTIALS OF BUSINESS ETIQUETTE

The first point of contact is crucial in establishing your brand. We discussed conversation as part of developing poise earlier. Let's dig deeper here.

First Meetings

Have you ever attended a meeting and had no idea who some of the other people attending were—what their role in the organization was or what their contribution would be? Here is how you can avoid that uncomfortable, unprofessional situation.

Introductions

When entering into a meeting or a meal situation, make sure you have greeted the participants and introduced yourself before you sit down, so there is no mystery about who you are. If you are already at the meeting, when introducing someone who joins you, usually the name of the person with higher authority is stated first. For example, "Mr. White, I would like to introduce Jane Clements, our marketing director. Jane, this is Mr. White, the XYZ Company president." Then go further and tell the president what Jane does for the company; knowing a person's role will help someone ease into conversation. Remembering names is always challenging—I never forget a face, but to this day names do still escape me—so use whatever tricks help jog your memory.

Handshaking

I promise, it is no accident that the U.S. president always has a picture taken while shaking hands with a foreign dignitary. The handshake and body language in these situations sometimes provide insight into or even define the relationship. Never underestimate a handshake; it can define your personal brand. A proper handshake requires facing shoulder to shoulder, with hand open and thumb extended upward for a true open palm (see Figure 1).

You meet palm to palm with the other person, giving a couple of pumps up and down, and keeping your elbows in—and that should do the job.

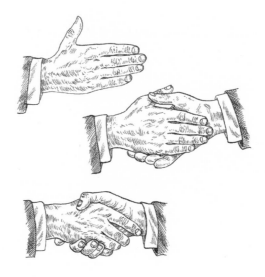

Figure 1: The Handshake

When a handshake is weak, turned sideways, or even omitted, it sends a signal to the other person. It may represent a lack of confidence or being timid. Men especially are sometimes scared to firmly grasp a female's hand to shake. I assure you, it is appropriate in a business setting (so long as it's not a bone crusher!). I will never forget how once, after I demonstrated the appropriate way to shake hands, a fifty-year-old man raised his hand and confessed that he had always been uncomfortable shaking a woman's hand. He had been in sales for twenty years. It is never too late to learn!

Eye signals

Ah yes, the eyes—the windows to the soul. Revealing as it is, eye contact can be one of the most powerful techniques for using poise to build your brand—as long as you follow proper etiquette. I remember my mother telling me, when I was a young girl, to stop staring at people when I was in church. Knowing how to keep your eyes in check is essential. Keep in mind the "business zone"—at the eyebrow level—and remember to look slightly away every now and then so as not to stare overtly. In some social situations, eyes focus on the mouth area, as some people read lips while they listen, but this can appear too flirty. Looking below the chin is a simple *no*, and believe me, women sure know when that is happening. Be very aware of what I call "eye streaming": looking people up and down, from head to toe. When people come to your house and you greet them at the door, how would you feel if instead of focusing on you, they let their eyes roam the walls and furniture to see what your house is like? It is off-putting. Stay focused on the face.

Figure 2: Eye signals

Personal zone

Speaking to someone while standing too close can be incredibly uncomfortable. Consider the other person's personal space, and stay at least six to ten inches away (See Figure 3). Be in tune with the distance you use when sitting next to someone (or across from them, behind them, etc.). I once had a boss who was incredibly friendly and usually made me feel comfortable, but when he came to my office, he would come behind my desk and look down while talking to me. He did not mean to intimidate—that was not his style. But it made me very uncomfortable, because I felt trapped and it was difficult to discuss things while looking straight up.

Figure 3: Personal distance

PRESENCE PRACTICE

Write down answers to the following questions as you consider them.

How many people do you physically come into contact with at work? How much time is spent on a one-on-one basis versus at a larger meeting? How much time do you spend at your work computer on e-mail or other business correspondence?

If the computer time far outweighs the personal time, make a clear and conscious effort to build a calendar that includes meeting people for one-on-ones, coffee, lunch, and so forth. Consider especially the folks you wish to build relationships with or you would like as mentors.

Events

For receptions, parties, and meet and greets, a simple, often overlooked etiquette gesture is the RSVP: *Répondez s'il vous plaît,* French for "Respond, please." No matter the event to which you have been invited, a response is crucial; it shows that you care about the invitation. Remember the story at the start of this chapter, regarding the employee who did not RSVP? Don't be the one left off the list for the next event. If you are the one building the invite, in addition to including the who, what, when, and where, never forget to answer the dress code and RSVP questions, giving your guests a road map for the event.

Mingling

When attending any event, look for the hosts/hostesses and acknowledge your appreciation for being invited; the same applies when you depart. If you are the host, stay near the entry to greet your guests and give direction. Networking at an event is about setting some small goals. Before attending a networking event, set a goal to meet a specific number of people. Your goal will help guide you, especially if you do not know many people attending. If you truly do not know anyone, swiftly and calmly introduce yourself to a few people; you will be surprised how many folks will be glad that you broke the ice.

Dining

When it comes to business dining, the goal is to navigate conversation in such a way that no one notices you are eating. The most important technique for developing poise during a meal is to understand how the meal is to be served and how the utensils are to be used. At banquets, it is easy to make mistakes when people become confused about which is their bread plate, their water glass, and so forth. Studying the following diagram will help you remember what each piece is for.

Figure 4: Dinnerware

The simple BMW (bread, meal, water) formula will come to your aid. Utensils always begin from the outside, so work your way in as the courses progress. Remove your napkin first and place it on your lap; wipe the corners of your mouth when needed. The water glass is always closest to the plate; moving out, find the white wine glass, then red wine, and finally champagne.

When eating, cut and take one bite at a time, and fully chew your food before you reach for your water glass. Always pass the bread and condiments if they are closest to you. Signal to the waiter that you are finished by placing your utensils like the hands of a clock in the 10:20 position. Fork and knife tips are at the 10 and ends are at the 20 position.

Dining do's and don'ts

Your poise at the dining table will make others comfortable and add to the overall pleasure of the dining experience. Follow this short list of table manners to ensure that you and those around you enjoy the meal—and that you project the right image while maintaining your brand.

- DO introduce yourself to the host and thank them for the invitation.
- DO introduce yourself to those you are seated near.
- DO be aware of your posture at the table, sitting straight in the chair.
- DO cover your hand over a lemon wedge when you squeeze the juice into a beverage.
- DO chew all your food using small bites before you sip your beverage.
- DO use your napkin to wipe the corners of your mouth.
- DON'T complain about the menu served at a business meal.
- DON'T reach across the table.

- DON'T push your plate away when you are finished; use the 10:20 position.
- DON'T put your elbows on the table.
- DON'T talk with your mouth full.
- DON'T pick up your silverware if it has dropped on the floor.
- DON'T lick your fingers, use your napkin.

Cross-cultural sensitivity

People often ask me about what to do as a host in cross-cultural situations. When you're facing a specific situation or someone from a particular culture, you can consult many wonderful books that dissect etiquette in each country, and the Internet is another fabulous resource for quick information. When planning for international events, I follow another acronym— CCPM, for "country, comfort, preferences, and message"—to ensure that I've covered everything.

Country: Establish what norms and values are expected by learning about the person's culture and what is appropriate. Is shaking hands acceptable? What is the best way to handle business card presentation? These sorts of practices vary by country, and it's important to make the effort to understand them.

Comfort: Consider how far the person has traveled, whether he/she might be experiencing jet lag, how to plan an itinerary around meals and rest, and what you can do to make him/her comfortable.

Preferences: What food preferences, religious restrictions, and such might the person have?

Message: Think about what message you should be sending—how formal is the event or meeting? What level of authority does the person have?

Hopefully, this acronym will help guide you with your next international guest.

Communications

There are a myriad of communication tools, but have you ever stepped back to review whether you are using them effectively or the way that they are meant to be used?

E-mail etiquette

E-mail was designed essentially for short, memolike messages, and yet I see a recurring theme of clients being overwhelmed with hundreds of e-mails a day. We have lost the human touch, the professional presence of face-to-face meetings. Instead we hide behind our computers, spewing direction after direction, and sometimes your intentions can be misread. When your e-mails replace discussion and you're sending fifty one-line thoughts a day that pile up in the recipient's inbox, you are burdening people.

Use your common sense when it comes to "netiquette." My best advice is to avoid writing lengthy epistles; a long e-mail is an indicator that you may need a face-to-face meeting instead. Know the difference between the two types of contact; often it depends on the subject. Ask yourself, *Should I send an e-mail, or should I call/meet?*

If you have to use e-mail, use the following e-mail format as a guideline:

To: _____

From: _____

Subject: _____

Greeting _____

      Point #1 _____

      Point #2 _____

      Point #3 _____

Closure _____

Contact Information _____

Figure 6: E-mail format

In addition to brevity, pay attention to your font size and your use of boldface words and capitalization, because believe it or not, words can scream. I worked for an executive once who always used caps, and we in the office always thought he was mad at us; the truth was, he was a poor typist, and with all caps he came across all wrong.

Finally, don't forget that *everything* in an e-mail becomes the property of the company. If you are sending personal memos, jokes, questionable photos, and such, you could be nailed to the wall for impropriety, with no way to defend yourself.

Social media

Social media is a beautiful thing, but like eating too much candy that can make you ill, using social media too much can jeopardize your personal brand. Manage wisely the time you spend on social media; when people find you on Facebook or Twitter 24/7, they might perceive that you are bored or have no life away from the computer. Sure, people want to hear from you—even business colleagues—but sharing every waking moment of your life (*Having coffee at Starbucks, Just went to the grocery store*, etc.) becomes annoying to others. This kind of trivial minutia does not add substance to your brand. Avoid using social media like a personal diary, announcing when you are angry, upset, depressed, and so forth. Anytime you display your message, keep it neutral and consistent; otherwise you may appear lonely and moody, which isn't professional and won't help you develop your brand.

Remember, while an online life is a necessary part of today's interaction, face time is still vital.

✦ ✦ ✦

Your mastery of business etiquette will add immensely to the personal brand you have already begun to build through the power of poise. But there is one last aspect to protocol, and that is the etiquette you need to employ in your everyday contacts: touchpoint etiquette.

PRO SCENARIO: MASTERING BUSINESS ETIQUETTE

Judy is the director of sales for a small company. She manages a team of five sales managers: Rob, Janice, Dan, Betsy, and Ellen. Under Judy's strict guidance, they all work very hard, but one of her managers has really helped the team achieve its best month yet. She sends an e-mail:

> Dear Team,
>
> Congratulations to Rob on helping the company reach our highest-revenue-producing month ever. I would also like to mention the work of Rob's coworkers, Janice, Dan, and Betsy, for having good months.
>
> Please don't interpret this news to mean that you can get lazy now. ;) We need to keep up the good work; our goals for the upcoming months are WAY higher than they were previously. If you didn't make your goals this time, please see me if u need help.
>
> Kindly,
>
> Judy

The fifth member of Judy's team, Ellen, is horrified by Judy's e-mail. Judy embarrassed her not only by leaving her off the list, but also by drawing attention to the fact that she didn't make her goals this time around. Meanwhile, Judy thought she was offering help, and her inclusion of an emoticon and informal spelling were intended to insert real-life emotion and friendly gestures.

What did Judy do wrong?

What should Judy have done?

What lessons can you apply?

For my responses to these questions, visit my website, www.peggynoestevens.com.

SKILL #3
DEVELOPING TOUCHPOINT ETIQUETTE

Etiquette is important at every organizational touchpoint: with your co-workers, your clients, your vendors, and everyone else with whom you come into contact. Improving your understanding of touchpoint etiquette will enable you to develop poise and build your brand.

Mistakes in touchpoint etiquette are all too common and are likely familiar to you. For example, when is the last time you actually apologized to someone? Ego certainly gets in the way, and sometimes even when we know that we've made a mistake, we avoid admonition by avoiding the people we offended. I see this all the time in the workplace—a sweeping under the rug of sorts. Great etiquette will always lead you back to the person or group that was wronged so you can offer a simple apology. People will value your sincerity and appreciate the gesture. What's more, they will come away with the feeling that you have integrity and self-awareness.

BASIC GUIDELINES

The fundamental elements of showing good manners and maintaining positive relationships should become second nature as you strive to build and preserve your brand. Never allow yourself to do the following:

- Lose your composure.
- Lose your temper at the smallest issue.
- Speak during an entire meeting without allowing others to voice their opinions.
- Arrive at a meeting late and/or unprepared.
- Appear visibly stressed and hurried, as if you're spinning out of control.
- Make excuses, be quick to blame others, or fail to embrace accountability.
- Leave long voice mails and e-mails when an issue should be handled in person.

If these actions show professional immaturity, those that follow show the opposite: maturity, professionalism, and integrity. Always do the following:

- Be willing to welcome new people cordially.
- Ask what more you could do for someone.
- Greet people and introduce them before a meeting or meal begins.
- Send thank-you notes and follow up with people.
- Be on time.
- Clearly express yourself without losing emotional control.
- Engage others regarding their opinions, and listen for obstacles.
- RSVP to an invite, or respond to an e-mail.
- Keep your door open as much as possible to show that you are approachable.

ETIQUETTE WITH YOUR CUSTOMERS AND VENDORS

Although many don't recognize it as such, etiquette is crucial when dealing with individuals outside your organization. Use the basic guidelines described above when connecting with customers and vendors; these techniques are designed to develop your touchpoint etiquette skills with important contacts both within and outside of your own company.

Customers

Because I come from a hospitality background, it is ingrained in me to always go above and beyond service expectations—to deliver results to the client with a sense of urgency. But for some people, the need to go above and beyond is not so obvious. Many people receive countless hours of sales training, for example, yet lack the core foundation in touchpoint etiquette to support their personal brand and actually close the deal. Basic and even advanced mistakes are made due to a lack of knowledge about the behavior and treatment customers expect.

I planned a field visit with a client and a local sales representative while working for a major corporation. During lunch I noticed that the salesperson was increasingly uncomfortable: He seemed to be trying to figure out the china, glass, and silverware landscape. He was awkward in conversation. At the end of our meal, he asked who should pick up the bill, he or I—right in front of our client! I remember thinking to myself, *We need to roll back to some basics to ensure that all sales reps are comfortable conducting busi-ness.* Deciding who should pay the bill when there are two people from the same company is easy. The person with the higher authority and budget is the one who should pay the bill. If that is not the policy in your company, then discuss it before the meal to avoid a mishap.

You may have all the technical training you can mus-ter, but it's polish and gravitas that will set you apart from the competition.

The word *charisma* comes from the Greek *khárisma*, which means "gift." The truth is that not everyone has the natural gift of a magnetic persona; etiquette supports and aids those without much inherent cha-risma in making a positive effect on clients.

Too often employees forget—or perhaps fail to ever realize—that they are a first point of contact for customers. Think about it as a make-or-break moment; when a potential customer might choose your company (or choose to walk away forever) according to a single interaction with you as the company's representative, *everything* counts. That includes an e-mail, a phone conversation or voice mail, your handshake, certain nonverbal ges-tures you might make, and any number of other points—even down to the ringtone on your cell phone. Every moment you are in contact with the client, you are on stage. I have seen the best salespeople go down in flames during a presentation or a dinner meeting because they did not have a com-manding presence or they appeared too "junior" in their professionalism.

On the other hand, etiquette can trigger your customers' confidence in you. Knowing how to hold yourself and how to act can create a calming effect for both you and your customer—no more guessing how much to leave for the tip or wondering whether to follow up with a client. Etiquette allows a certain fluidity to reach the workplace.

Part of the professional presence is accepting people for who they are, despite their distractions, and looking for even the smallest positive attributes. But your clients do not have to follow this protocol—you might wish they all did, but they don't. They can evade, skip over, and cancel an appointment with you at the drop of a hat. For this reason, I have learned to become familiar with all the people who stem from the main client—the receptionist, the secretary, peers—as they can help you connect with the person you need to meet.

It is only natural that customers will spend more time with individuals who are not distracting or offensive. We all tend to avoid people who irritate us, even in the business world and even though we still need to work with those people. It is human nature. People do business with people they like—this is a famous sales mantra from way back. So make sure to turn on the charm, make it genuine, and be professional with clients at every potential touchpoint.

VENDORS

When I began my own company, I remember creating a "hit list" of potential clients who might require my consulting services. My jobs over the years have taken me from event planning to global marketing, so you can imagine the diversity in vendors. As I developed the list, I decided to contact all those past vendors to let them know where I was and what I was doing. I never expected more from this notice of change. Instead, I was overwhelmed with support; I was given leads and contacts, and I actually partnered with a past vendor on my very first contract.

Why was I received so well? It may have something to do with what I was told over and over: "You were so great to work with" and "You always treated my staff well." I had displayed a professional presence that they remembered, and because of my personal brand, I was rewarded by their support.

I partnered with a company on a project where our mutual client yelled and created an incredibly uncomfortable work environment. It was a horrible display to witness. The last straw for me was how the client treated the other vendor's employees like stepchildren in a fairy tale, continually berating them. It was despicable. When I asked the president of the company how she allowed such behavior from a client, she replied, "We need the money."

Sorry, folks, but when the same client thought he could treat my employees as he did the other vendor's, I put a halt to that behavior. No, I did not go in kicking and screaming. Instead I calmly outlined my expectations and left the issue on the table. That way, it was for him to decide whether we were right for his company or not.

I was surprised when he kept us on. He later told me

the reason he liked to work with me was that I was not afraid of him. Go figure. All I know is, I did what was best for my employees, despite the consequences. Vendors matter, you matter, we all matter—let's act like it.

Touchpoint etiquette builds your brand out from your organization to include a wider network of contacts. It is a crucial element of developing the poise and business etiquette you will need to establish your brand.

PRO SCENARIO: DEVELOPING TOUCHPOINT ETIQUETTE

Kelly has worked at a popular restaurant for several years. It is an extremely busy environment that involves a lot of people to keep it operating, and Kelly has done a great job of managing it all. Kelly has a reputation for being hardworking and loyal. She is great with customers and great with her staff. She takes pride in ensuring that the restaurant's guests receive a high-quality meal—and this can lead to problems. Kelly's vendors sometimes have a hard time pleasing her. With a lot of pressure to deliver on her customers' expectations and her own, Kelly often finds herself in arguments with the restaurant's delivery people, salesmen, produce farmers, and so forth. She just doesn't have the time to spend worrying about their schedules and issues with their products—she wants what she wants.

Eventually, Kelly is presented with the opportunity to own her own restaurant. She is confident that she can assemble the best team in the business and that, knowing she stands for quality, her customers will follow her. She is right. A lot of people want to see her succeed; she has worked hard, and she deserves it.

As she's preparing for the opening of her new restaurant, Kelly calls on the vendors she knows. Sadly, Kelly doesn't receive the same well-wishes from them. Some don't even return her call. Word has spread that Kelly has started this new venture, and while vendors would love her business, they just aren't eager to work with her.

Kelly perseveres and finds new vendors who are ready and willing. She's all set to open. Her staff is in place, and customers are lined up to receive a warm greeting from Kelly herself. Traffic in the restaurant that first night is great, but as with all new restaurants, after a few months it slows down. Kelly isn't prepared for this, so she panics. She puts tremendous pressure on her vendors to give her lower and lower prices for smaller orders and to make deliveries at difficult times of the day. This makes it difficult for her smaller vendors to serve their other customers well, so a number of them are forced to stop doing business with her. Eventually, Kelly has to close her restaurant.

What happened to Kelly's business?

What could Kelly have done differently?

What lessons can you apply?

For my responses to these questions, visit my website, www.peggynoestevens.com.

PART I
SUMMARY

Professional presence is not about rules and rigidity; it is about respect and thoughtfulness for the people around you. Adopting a great sense of protocol and understanding appropriate etiquette can help you exude masterful poise and business professionalism. When you are confident and self-aware in your personal comportment, and dignified and considerate in your approach to business relationships, you are creating a positive image that radiates outward and affects all your interactions. Without establishing this basic framework for your personal brand, as you begin to build your professional image you will find it is like building a house with no foundation. And it all starts with protocol.

PART II: PERSONAL

Be fearless on feedback.

OVERVIEW

In today's competitive market, every social interaction is a potential win for your personal brand. Whether it's in a client's office, at a restaurant, or on the soccer field, making a good first impression isn't just important—it's the foundation of a successful career. Now that you have learned about the power of *protocol* and mastered the essentials, you are ready to discover the *personal* dimension of the professional presence. As you develop poise and learn to manage etiquette, you must also develop the personal skills that will enable you to thrive in business and social situations. Remember, poise is about how you project yourself, whereas personal skill is about how you work inwardly. As we examine these personal factors that influence your brand, they can be broken into two categories: your personal appearance and your personal life.

I know what you are thinking: *I am not so shallow that I judge people by their appearance!* But it actually has nothing to do with being shallow. It has to do with human nature and the wealth of advertisements and sensory information we have gathered though the years from society, family, and culture. We humans might do our best to avoid stereotypical behavior, but like it or not, we sometimes judge books by their covers.

Let me share some true examples, with an exercise I use during image class training. I hold up each of these photos, one by one, and ask the class a series of questions:

Figure 7: Image class photos

What do I do for a living?

Am I successful?

How would you describe my personality?

Would you believe what I say?

I receive an immediate response from the crowd, describing (sometimes in great detail) which of these people are successful and what they are all about. Granted, this is the first exercise of the training session, so the class actually is getting acquainted with me as well. So my next question is pretty straightforward: "How many of you, as I began this presentation, looked at what I was wearing? How many of you began to wonder about my personality after my bio was read and I stood up in front of you?"

It is at that very moment—the first touchpoint—that we begin to identify human nature. I can't apologize for the automatic response, nor can I take credit. I just know that we humans do respond, either positively or negatively. The point is, no matter how sincerely we intend not to judge the book by its cover, there is a part of us that inevitably does just that, even if it is subliminally. Often, we underestimate the importance of our appearance—and even misjudge the impression we make on others.

We are surrounded by thousands of visual cues that influence our decisions, many of which are subliminal. Whether we like it or not, visual cues in various types of advertising, how celebrities dress, the speech of political figures, and the behavior of business executives are what shape and form perceptions and opinions, both positive and negative. This megatrend applies to you, too. Everyone around you is conditioned to respond to visual cues, so the impressions you create through your visual style have a major impact—perhaps more today than ever before. Appearances sway others and their perceptions, so you need to manage how the impression you make affects your personal brand in the workplace and in the rest of your life.

In business and social settings, how you affect the five senses of the people you meet has a dramatic effect on how they perceive your brand.

Early studies conclude that 93 percent of your communication is nonverbal. This clearly demonstrates the importance of appearance in defining your personal brand.

The following skills will teach you how to develop your brand by improving your personal appearance—from your grooming habits to the clothes you choose—and organizing your personal life:

Skill #4: Personal Grooming

Skill #5: Dressing Your Brand

Skill #6: Managing Your Personal Life

SKILL #4
PERSONAL GROOMING

Do you remember some people by their perfume? By the state of their fingernails? By their hairstyle? Of course you do. In return, your personal grooming habits affect the senses of everyone you meet: their sight, smell, touch, and hearing, all except perhaps taste (unless you happen to travel to a truly strange part of the world). Your personal grooming—your appearance—is perhaps the most important factor in making a good first impression, and as I have mentioned previously, creating positive first impressions is one key to building a successful brand.

Many of us have a certain routine for our personal grooming, but as we become accustomed to the workplace, often we forget how important it is to pay attention to the routine. We forget how we appear to others and especially how we appear to people we have not yet met. Once our personal grooming standards slip, we run the risk of degrading our brand with both our current and our future colleagues. A clean overall appearance will keep you looking bright and well put together. And when this is part of people's perception of you, it can make all the difference to your success in business—and in life.

GROOMING TECHNIQUES

Here are some suggested techniques for using personal grooming to improve your brand.

Hair

Both men and women need to keep their hair neat and trimmed while in the workplace. The length and cut do not matter as much as the cleanliness and overall appearance of the hair. Remember, too, that extreme hairstyles and even gestures such as constantly pushing your hair back from your eyes may have a negative impact on your brand, because they become distractions to the viewer.

When deciding on a style and a stylist, both men and women have a multitude of options. It is not a bad idea to start with a consultation, where you talk to the stylist about color and how best to frame your face. Deciding on these two things will help build a comfort zone before you attempt to change or enhance your hairstyle.

Facial Hair

As we've established, eyes are the windows to the soul, and eye contact is a crucial element of conversation. Eyebrows frame that important piece. For women, waxing, shaping, or filling in your eyebrows to give balance to your face is a useful way to improve your look. Likewise, facial hair for men—whether it's a mustache, beard, or goatee—should be kept in shape.

Perfume/Cologne

Have you ever hugged someone and found that, an hour later, you could still smell the person? Whether you find cologne or perfume delightful or not so much, know how to wear it in a business setting. Apply to the upper arms (not the wrists) so you avoid leaving your mark during a handshake. Another safe spot is your chest (not your neck or face). Not sure if you've overdone it? If possible, ask someone in your home to do the smell test before you leave for work. Remember, some people are greatly affected by the smell of perfume—and not in a good way. It can become literally nauseating, especially when you are traveling together or are in close quarters. People will actually avoid you because of the smell—and of course, this is the reverse of your intention.

Hand Washing

It is very important to keep your hands and nails clean, not only for the sake of appearance but also to avoid spreading germs in the workplace. When you have a cold (or you know that someone else does), you may refrain from shaking hands by saying, "Excuse me, but I've been under the weather. Please forgive me for not shaking your hand." People actually appreciate this.

Proportion and Mental Walk-through

As you consider your appearance, be aware of how others see you. The following chart provides a critical list of cues to check when it comes to your personal appearance and how others perceive you. Use this helpful list before you walk out the door to begin your day.

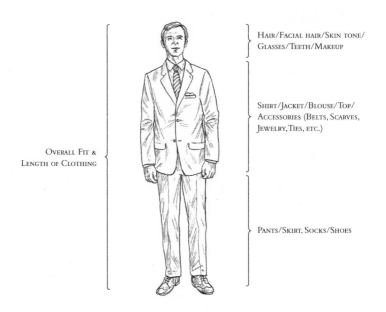

Hair/Facial hair/Skin tone/
Glasses/Teeth/Makeup

Shirt/Jacket/Blouse/Top/
Accessories (Belts, Scarves,
Jewelry, Ties, etc.)

Overall Fit &
Length of Clothing

Pants/Skirt, Socks/Shoes

Figure 8: Proportion and checklist

Rest

Do you know your body clock well? Are you aware of how many hours of sleep you truly need to function well? Most people require seven to eight hours of sleep each night. There are many weekends, I assure you, when I ferry my kids from event to event, leaving me exhausted by Sunday and not feeling rested for the week ahead. If I find myself in that state, I make a mental note about what I like to call "catch-up sleep" and take naps on Sunday, go to bed an hour earlier than normal, or allow myself to sleep in a little during the week to "catch up."

Lack of sleep affects your patience level and alertness; you're more likely to become sharp or cross when you are tired. But that's not all. We all have seen how lack of sleep can physically affect your appearance: peaked skin, puffy eyes with dark circles. Cumulatively for the week, you want to target a certain number of hours of sleep according to your body clock and what works for you. Always try to reach that balance by the end of the week.

My advice about rest is for everyone except new parents—nothing I could say or do will balance your first few weeks with an infant. I remember with my first son, Utah, who had colic, I would stand by the coffeepot in the morning almost in tears because the coffee was not brewing fast enough! If you don't get enough rest, you will be one of those people constantly yawning, sleepy, and hanging around the coffeepot—not a great image. Worse are the people who complain about their lack of sleep from the night before, as if you wish to hear about their sleep patterns. Don't complain or try to fix things with caffeine or other tricks. Get the right amount of sleep in the first place so you don't have this problem!

Personal grooming affects the senses of every person we meet, and it has just as much of an impact as our personal wardrobe does, which we'll address in Skill #5. Your personal wardrobe is not about being pretty or perfect; it is about improving your personal brand by enhancing the best possible you and focusing on areas that are completely controllable.

PRESENCE PRACTICE

Browse through five very different types of magazines that display clothing, hair, and makeup. Cut out anything that you feel reflects an inspiration for your own image, and begin a file folder. I like to use this exercise with clients to help unveil their goals and work toward the image that best suits them. Designers do this when they want to decorate your home; they try to understand your color palette, style of furniture, whether you are classic, modern, rustic, etc. The same applies to your overall appearance.

OFFICE GROOMING

Your personal environment is just as important as your personal appearance when it comes to developing your personal brand. Naturally, the environment that reflects most on your personal brand is the office. The following is a list of items to consider as you create or "groom" your office environment.

Overall Appearance

What "first impression" does your office give? Is it neat and professional? Who in your company has a great office? What can you do to emulate that space?

Furniture and Accessories

Is all the furniture in your office in good condition? If not, see whether repairs or replacements can be made. If your space permits, add a nice side table or a lamp to make the decor seem more finished.

Clutter

Are there stacks of paper, folders, and publications lying around? In today's electronic world, there is simply no need for a lot of paper. Try to minimize the amount of it in your office. Those documents you do need should be in neat files or storage bins, and you should keep them only as long as necessary. If this is a challenge for you, block out a date on your calendar once a month or once a quarter to purge unnecessary paperwork.

Personal Items

Keep personal items to a minimum. The message you want to convey is that you are at work to *work*, not to promote your favorite activity or team. If you do have some personal items, such as family photos, they should be well framed, and neatly displayed.

Artwork

Attractive, well-framed, noncontroversial artwork can really improve office decor and give the impression that you care about having a nice environment for clients and visitors. Artwork can be an expression of your personality, but ask for a second (and third) opinion before hanging it, so you can be sure that it will not offend people or give them the wrong impression.

Screen Saver

Your computer wallpaper should be professional as well. PowerPoint presentations where the screen saver is projected onto a large screen should not display vacation imagery, kids at the beach, and so forth. Again, keeping personal-themed items to a minimum is suggested.

Books

Display only work-related books in your office. Don't put books on the shelves only for show, as this might seem pretentious and could backfire on you. A book can be a great way to start an interesting business conversation with a guest—but only if you have actually read it!

Lighting

Make sure your entire office, including your desk area, is well lit. Not only will a well-lit office make you more productive, but it will also create a more comfortable environment for visitors. If possible, let in natural light and avoid fluorescent bulbs.

Awards

Only display awards that are relevant to your current (or future) job. By all means, hang your plaque on the wall if it is recent and will leave a good impression on colleagues, clients, and superiors. Outdated or nonprofessional awards, on the other hand, send the message that you are hanging on to past accomplishments rather than looking toward your next move up. Do not display awards that are not work related.

Music

If you need background music while you work, make sure it is kept at a very low level so you do not disturb your neighbors. Turn the music off if anyone comes to your office, as it may be a distraction to conversation. It is best to agree collectively as an office what station should be set on the dial. If you want your own music, earphones are a must.

Odor

In workspaces without windows or good ventilation, the air can become stale. Make sure you discard food containers away from your office, not in your own rubbish bin. Don't keep items like your gym bag in your office. If necessary, use an unscented or odor-neutralizing spray—very sparingly, so it is not offensive to others.

Vehicle

While your car is not technically part of your office, you may drive it to work or to work-related functions. A car is an extension of yourself, and as such, it should reflect your standard of grooming. It should be clean and well kept, inside and out, at all times. If you have to keep your kids' soccer gear in the car, use the trunk! Remove food wrappers and cups as soon as possible to avoid odors and spills.

+ + +

The point of this chapter is this: Review your personal grooming choices as if for the first time, looking objectively. Then view some of the suggestions here. If you are comfortable with where you are, great. If, however, there are areas that could benefit from increased concentration, then take advantage of the advice in this chapter. Grooming habits are low-hanging fruit on your quest to developing your personal brand.

SKILL #5
DRESSING YOUR BRAND

As we learned in our discussion about poise (Skill #1), clothing is your most powerful nonverbal communication tool. What you wear makes an overwhelming contribution to your sense of poise—and to the sense others get about you. Think of your clothing image as a simple challenge in shaping perceived impressions. The cues sent by clothing are both visual and emotional; they elicit unconscious reactions in those we meet and influence a great many decisions—as minor as being chosen to represent your company at a business lunch, or as major as being interviewed for a new job.

More than you may realize, your clothing defines *your* brand, particularly within the environment of your workplace. You have to dress for your career overall, but you also have to dress appropriately for each setting you're in during the course of a day, week, or month. Managers also need to know how to handle issues of inappropriate attire; when one of your team members has a business clothing issue, you're the one who needs to deliver the message on behalf of the company.

I have coached countless employees and executives on their image and how dress affects it. One particular woman surfaces in my mind, however, when I think of how dress can transform a person—and a career. Gail worked in the IT department at a major corporation, and she was truly brilliant. I admired Gail for how serious she was about her career, especially at her young age.

Her employer saw great value in her knowledge, but unfortunately her superiors were not taking her as seriously as they should have. She failed to advance because her style was a roadblock in her professionalism. Even though she did stellar work, her appearance and lack of sophistication held her back. The initial impression she gave was unprofessional: stringy-looking long hair, circles under her eyes, a wardrobe that looked collegiate rather than one that reflected the serious businesswoman I knew she was.

It is not my job to make women look pretty and perfect. In fact, I would be the first in line to ridicule an image consultant for forcing professionals to look too sexualized in a business setting. My goal instead is to have men and women look the part and dress the best for their body shape and natural, God-given features.

We gave Gail a makeover, and lo and behold! Underneath the bushy eyebrows, stringy hair, and boxy clothes,

She presented as a fabulous, professionally groomed young executive. When she returned to the office after her transformation, her co-workers stopped in their tracks. They were surprised and impressed. My favorite response: a colleague asking her if she had been on vacation!

By understanding what choices are effective for your body, the professional situation, and your personal comfort, you'll also save money and time by buying the clothes you need and avoiding the clothes you thought you needed (but don't). With this skill, we'll help you determine what kind of clothing is right for you, and how you can use clothing to improve your personal brand. The common thread that strings your look together, however, is your authenticity as you dress for various roles.

There are two key factors in dressing for your brand. The first factor is approachability; the second is style.

APPROACHABILITY

Why is *approachability* so important in business dress? Think about how long it would take you to answer the following question: Who in your office is the most approachable person? The image of that person probably flashed in your mind right away, along with a feeling of warmth and perhaps a list of positive words. This also holds at the other end of the spectrum: Those who are not approachable are easily described.

Approachability has to do with creating a comfort level that allows another person to enter into an honest dialogue with you. Why is it that some executives are so approachable, while the idea of having to exchange conversation with others creates a pit in your stomach?

The worst offenders are what I like to call the "screamers." These are the people who, at no matter what level, manage by intimidation and loudness rather than mental strength and leadership. Many times screamers support this image with their clothing: either too perfect suits and supercrisp shirts pressed beyond perfection, or a disheveled and sloppy ensemble. There is no "in between," because these folks are extreme.

When I think back over my career, it does not take long to recall the number of screamers I encountered. Sure, they got their way through coercion at times, but they also stacked up little respect among peers and employees. When screamers are revealed to upper-level management because they've forgotten to maintain their poise, their career is usually derailed.

Once, I was trying to impress a new boss. We were to meet one-on-one and outline our goals for the year. Later that day, we would also meet with staff members to discuss the plan. My boss had been with the company for quite some time and was always a first-class kind of guy, a quality-minded individual. I was certainly trying to look the part and, admittedly, went a little overboard. Not only did I wear my best suit, but I adorned it with iconic-label scarves, jewelry galore, and heels that could have pounded a nail in the wall. Nonetheless, my boss and I had a good get-together, and frankly, the staff meeting afterward was far from my mind.

As the staff meeting began, I sat by myself. I was surprised that during the course of the meeting no one really engaged me. At the time, I simply assumed they were tentative because I was new to the company. Later, my boss pulled me aside and said something that opened my eyes: I looked "expensive" and may have intimidated some of the others, so if I caught a bit of apprehensiveness from the staff, that could have been why.

I was confused by his remarks, but later they sank in, and I appreciated his coaching. I was not approachable. I had sat by myself, adorned with cocktail jewelry. Rather than make an effort to welcome conversation, I had expected everyone to come to me, since I had walked in with the boss and was a new employee.

After that conversation, I learned that loud jewelry, dramatic shoes, and excessive colors can put folks on the defensive. Effective presentation balances dignity and authority with accessibility.

The Elements of Approachability

Understanding your audience and the effect you desire to have on that audience is important when making choices about your wardrobe. Colors, fabrics, and the style you choose can all play a role.

Approachability isn't entirely about how you dress, though. Always enter a room with a smile or a friendly *Hello* and *Good morning.* Those in the room can sense your energy level simply by the entrance you make. If you are all business, then you will enter a room directly and take a seat quickly, symbolizing your readiness to start a meeting. For a more approachable entrance to a meeting, enter the room slowly, taking your time to greet people as they come in. If participants are coming to your office, then you may even stand up to greet them and sit somewhere other than at your desk during the meeting.

Audience

Always think of your audience and what might intimidate them. What is the message you need to convey? Is it serious or light-hearted? Good news or bad? Are you presenting a detailed financial report, or more general business results? What would make this audience understand your message? How comfortable do you want to make them feel?

I know a high-powered female cheif marketing officer who is truly a wonderful resource, a champion of women in business. She has an overwhelming amount of experience to share with others in regard to mentoring and career advancement. When she came to me, her issue was that she dressed so formally, with every hair numbered and in place (what I call the "everyday Wall Street" look), that the younger women were intimidated by her. Her workaholic personality and jet-set life showed in her appearance, and she actually became the last person other women would go to for advice, because they just didn't feel comfortable around her. To them, she was untouchable.

My advice to her came in the form of some questions: *Do you own a pair of jeans? Has your hair ever been in a ponytail?* I coached her in the opposite direction of most people—to come down a peg or two during staff meetings and social gatherings so the younger women felt more comfortable approaching her. I also encouraged her to reach out to others instead of expecting them to dial her up and ask her to go to lunch. In time, her standing with the younger women began to change, and she was able to establish better relationships and mentor-protégé connections because she became more approachable.

The opposite can apply as well. Another executive who played an important role in her company needed to dial up her too casual look. She felt that her employees were not taking her seriously. Although she wanted to be approachable, she also needed to balance her wardrobe to achieve the desired effect. She made some simple changes, moving from loose-fitting fabrics to a crisper style, but kept the colors soft so as not to appear too intense.

Color

When you want to appear approachable, a simple trick is to wear colors (yes, there might be more than one) that match your eyes. I always get a snicker when, during an image session, I ask the individual to reach for the mirror and look deeply at his or her own eyes. This immediately leads to an awkward moment, but the exercise is extremely effective. When I ask clients what colors they see, the response is usually only one color: brown, blue, or green.

But then I ask him/her, "What other colors do you see—the specks throughout, the ones that are not so dominant? How about the ring around your pupil that defines your eye color? What shade of white are the whites of your eyes?"Then the gates open as people begin to describe in detail the other shades and colors they see. Some are surprised to find that there are three or four colors and shades to their eyes.

Then I place in front of the client a color wheel, similar to the palette of an artist, with a rainbow of shades and colors. I ask the person to choose the shades most similar to those found in his/her eyes. These are the colors that person should look for when assembling a wardrobe.

You are most approachable when wearing the very same colors as those within your eyes. Following the psychology of this technique, when you want to appear more approachable, consider matching your wardrobe choice to your eye color. On the contrary, when you need to appear more formal and serious, wear darker colors and move away from your natural tones.

Fabric

Always avoid clothes and fabrics that are too stiff and crisp. When trying to appear more approachable, try not to look overpressed; don't give your shirts severe pointed collars and sharp edges. Use softer fabrics that drape, such as silk or poly blends, and try open collars and jackets, to accentuate your openness and bring out your lighter side.

Other tips

Here are some other tips for creating approachability and the desired emotional energy level with the right arrival and greeting:

- Arrive at least five minutes before the scheduled start. If you must be late, apologize briefly and be seated immediately.

- Limit the materials you carry with you, or bring something to carry them in so you are ready to shake hands.
- Keep personal articles to a minimum.
- Enter slowly and with confidence, but do not draw too much attention to yourself.
- Pause at the doorway and decide where you will sit, or ask a host for seating instruction.
- If time allows, introduce yourself to people you do not know.
- Settle in before taking refreshments, if possible, and avoid interruptions.
- Recognize your physical stance and be sure your posture is confidently upright, not slouching with rolled shoulders (as if you dread making an entrance).

STYLE

Many professionals find it hard to expand their thinking beyond their existing wardrobe, and many worry about lengthy and expensive shopping sessions. Forget the golden handcuffs created by fashion in the media; forget the ego boost or bust attached to clothing tags that describe size. Focus instead on the outcome: the goal of presenting your authentic personal style.

In addition to my experience with professionals aspiring to grow their careers, I can't overlook the number of women who seek out professional image enhancers after having stayed home to raise their children. Over the years, they may have lost touch with their personal style, and now they want to go back to a career they began building before parenthood interrupted.

The first step is to identify an aspirational image, the image you wish to convey. What are you going for? Do you want to convey an edgy, creative look, or is it important that you be seen as a serious businessperson? The next step is to understand your personal style, and finally you must calibrate the two. It may sound complicated, but I promise, the most difficult part is simply getting started. The following guidelines will help.

The Elements of Style

Dress code

Always be clear on the dress code for any occasion to avoid the possibility of being under- or overdressed. (Notice how this statement circles back to the business etiquette of invitations and making sure that dress code is included.)

Always dress on the more conservative side of whatever code your workplace follows, especially if that code is "business casual." There are days when I walk into the office of a very prestigious corporation only to find employees greeting me in dressy flip-flops (is there really such a thing?) and "stretch pants" (aka upgraded sweatpants). Casual dress takes on all kinds of interpretations, and I rely heavily on a company's HR folks to define its policy so there is no confusion. If your company has a dress code policy, ask for it by name. Be appropriate to the culture; it is simply a sign of respect for yourself and others.

Following are some basic dress code definitions for events in the workplace and beyond:

Business Casual or Smart Business Casual

MEN: Collared shirt (long-sleeved, buttoned shirt without a tie, or nice golf shirt); dress pants or pressed cotton trousers (khakis); coordinating leather belt and shoes (loafers) and dark socks

WOMEN: Tailored shirt or blouse, sweater or sweater set, or nice golf shirt; well-fitting, crisp pants or skirt (preferably in a solid, neutral color; skirts no shorter than just above the knee); closed-toe leather or fabric shoes with a reasonable heel height (no chunky or platform soles); hose optional (but suggested if skirts are knee length); fairly simple and conservative accessories and purse

Dressy Casual

MEN: Trousers and sports coat

WOMEN: Dressy pants and sweater or jacket

Cocktail Attire

MEN: Dark suit

WOMEN: Short, elegant dress

Semiformal or Business Formal

MEN: Dark suit for evening; dark or light suit for daytime

WOMEN: Tailored dressy suit or dress

Creative Black Tie

MEN: Modern twist on the tuxedo, such as a dark shirt with no tie

WOMEN: Cocktail dress, long dress, or dressy separates

Black Tie Optional or Black Tie Invited

MEN: Tuxedo or dark suit

WOMEN: Cocktail dress, long dress, or dressy separates

Black Tie or Formal

MEN: Tuxedo

WOMEN: Cocktail dress, long dress, or dressy separates

White Tie or Ultra Formal

MEN: Full tuxedo, including vest and white tie

WOMEN: Long dress or dressy evening separates

✦ ✦ ✦

I do wonder why people ignore or rebel against a company dress code—why some employees refuse to be persuaded by the company to adjust their look to meet the dress code. Believe me, on weekends you will find me in a baseball hat, jeans, and little or no makeup. I appreciate the more relaxed mode of business dress, as it is not always so comfortable to "dress up." I encourage you, however, to know the difference in how management typically treats employees who don't follow business etiquette. Rebels usually do not ascend to the top of the company, and if that is OK by you—great. Just know that you are the one in charge of that decision, and be aware of the consequences.

Clothing and fit

Always dress for the job you want, not the job you have. I constantly ask my clients what job they want next, and then pose a few questions about it: *What would be the persona of someone who had that job? What would be expected of your dress?* I especially encourage administrative assistants looking to move into other areas to dress professionally so as not to get "pigeonholed" in that role. Managers will take notice when the whole package is marketable.

Think of the millions of dollars spent in the packaging industry, with focus group after focus group laboring over color analysis, font style, and graphics. Why do companies and advertisers do this? Because they want to attract the consumer to their brand. When a position comes open within your company, can the company picture you in that position?

One thing that will help is always to wear clothes that fit. Many people avoid shopping for clothes because they can't seem to find the right fit. I strongly suggest that, no matter your size, you find a great tailor to work with. Your tailor will have your true measurements, so you can either purchase clothing and have it tailored later or select styles that the tailor can make for you. There is an old expression: *It's not what you wear, it's how you wear it.* The simple tailoring of clothing can essentially change the look of the outfit—and the perception of the whole package. If your clothing does not fit appropriately, you lose the edge you are attempting to create. Some simple tailoring can complete the look and accentuate your silhouette. Common mistakes when clothes are not tailored include the following:

- Sleeves are too long and hang over your hands.
- Pant hemlines drag.
- Poor-fitting waistlines cause you to pin or tighten a belt, so

there is extra fabric bunching around your midsection.

- Oversized jackets appear too boxy and ill constructed.

- Shoulders that hang beyond your shoulder line give you a slouched appearance.

- Too much fabric in the legs gives you the appearance of looking bigger than you are.

Accessories

Always skip chintzy accessories. For women, these include distracting bracelets and gaudy pins and scarves. For men, it would be ties or lapel pins with messages or hobbyist imagery, large belt buckles, and anything in the watch or key chain realm that does not express professionalism.

When considering how to accessorize an outfit, keep in mind the word *relate*. The most common mistake men make in dress is a lack of relatedness. Someone may dress in a sharp designer suit but still wear his running watch. These do not match; they do not *relate*. A woman may wear a feminine dress with lightweight fabric and pastel colors, but her shoes may be chunky and heavy-looking. Again, the items do not relate to each other.

A simple way to understand whether your clothes relate is to look in a full-length mirror *before* you leave home. Start at the top, with your hairstyle that day, and work your way down, taking note of your clothes, belt, shoes, jewelry, scarves, and so forth, to see if they all relate. If a more formal day is in the plan, all accessories should be formal in order to relate to the total look. If a more casual day is called for, then more casual accessories are the way to go.

Always ensure that briefcases, umbrellas, shoes, and business suitcases are timeless and in good repair. Sentimentality sometimes takes over, and professionals are tempted with a novelty umbrella or a briefcase that shows years of wear and tear. I remember one executive who traveled with an incredibly worn-out briefcase as if it were a badge commemorating his years of dedication to his job. Instead of the desired effect, people would comment that they could not believe, with all the money he made, that he would carry around such a tattered case.

Makeup

Women can give their look more vibrancy with the use of basic makeup. Outlandish makeup styles not only may be off-putting, but also take too much "face time" in front of the mirror each day. For years I complacently attempted a trial-and-error process, buying brand after brand, chasing colors that I thought were appropriate and following the trends (e.g., eyeliner inside the lower eyelid in the 1980s). It was not until I worked with a makeup artist and received a frank lesson on application that I learned what truly works—and what wasn't working for me at all.

There are a multitude of readily available makeup artists in any of your local department stores who can help you, and the same applies to most salons (though you might have to pay for the latter). When I take my clients to a makeup professional, I request an analysis of the person's facial bone structure, the pigment of her skin, and her hairstyle to determine the correct products. My first goal is to understand my client's particular needs. For example, if her face looks tired and unexpressive, we will work on how to use concealer and eye makeup to accentuate her eyes. If the client has rosacea (skin that becomes very ruddy), then we may work on determining a foundation that will tone down the red. A pale and pasty skin tone will require a focus on blush and foundation. As with all other elements of style, it's important to choose makeup according to what is most appropriate for you—your facial characteristics, your professional situation, and your overall image.

The true takeaways when considering what makeup to wear are to be realistic about the time required for application and to be true to the ultimate goal of looking healthy and vibrant.

Fixes and repairs

Never muddle through an important business occasion with a clothing "fail." If you have an emergency—a rip, a spill or stain, a forgotten tie or jacket, a lost item—be creative about resolving it. Try to buy or borrow what you need, even if you have to find a way to slip out of the office and get it done. Big-time failures do not happen every day, but little problems do crop up—and sometimes it's the little things that get noticed.

Here are a few suggestions for things you can do to prepare in a pinch:

- Always keep a change of clothes in the office or your car (and replace or update it when necessary) so that should a spill or a tear occur, a quick change is available. As soon as you begin a new job, stock your clothing emergency drawer with whatever is appropriate to the dress code—an extra blouse, a tie, a belt, what have you.
- Always pack a backup outfit if you are traveling, no matter what the trip entails.

- When traveling by airplane, always pack miniature toiletries and one change of clothing (the essentials) in your carry-on baggage, just in case. It takes only one experience with lost luggage to make this a habit for life.
- Put together a small repair kit—safety pins, stain-removal stick, lint brush, toothbrush—to keep in your desk for those quick brush-up moments.

During one hilarious business trip (well, it's funny *now*) that I took to Milan with a group of my peers, I was unfortunate enough to be caught off guard when my luggage was lost. (Luggage lost by an airline? How unusual!) A male colleague had the same misfortune, and the two of us had just a few hours to scurry through the city in search of a week's worth of professional clothing—in a foreign country, no less. Luckily, we were in stylish Milan! Still, this experience forced me to think about the true meaning of "bare essentials," and now I always carry with me the basics to rebuild a business wardrobe—just in case.

Never assume that your colleagues don't notice what you're wearing. The second you walk in the door, your style begins to have an impact on the brains of those who are present. Mental notes are made, consciously or not, in regard to not only your entrance, your timeliness, and your energy level, but also your appearance. The significance of the first five minutes of any encounter should never be underestimated, because it can set the stage for the rest of your day or evening—and maybe even your career.

Use your common sense when dressing for any type of event. Think ahead to the occasion and what impression you wish to deliver. Follow the dress code of your office, even when someone tells you it is not necessary. There's always something to gain by maintaining a professional appearance.

BASIC GUIDELINES

In short, here are the guidelines that will help you dress for any situation and look your best, no matter where you are. Whether you are a man or a woman, when seeking to dress for success, consider the following four questions:

1. *Purpose:* What am I trying to say with my clothing?
2. *Color:* Where do I fall on the approachability spectrum, from accessible and welcoming to formal and powerful?
3. *Texture:* What are the best fabrics and weights for my body type and for the situation?
4. *Fit:* Do my clothes hang on me, or are they too tight?

When it comes to conveying professionalism with your clothing choices, the issues are universal. No matter if you are a man or a woman, the boss or an intern, style matters.

PRESENCE PRACTICE

Do a complete inventory of your wardrobe—a pro scenario of yourself. After the general inventory, take a second look. Try on key clothing that you rely upon on a daily basis. Stand in front of the mirror and judge for yourself how your clothes fit, or ask for a tailor's opinion. Where are the problem areas—too long in the sleeves, too short in the hem, and so forth? How do your pants fit through the waistline? Does the jacket hang in line with the profile of your body?

 ## PRO SCENARIO: DRESSING YOUR BRAND

Mary Ellen is a talented, personable, twenty-five-year-old engineer with stellar credentials who recently joined a midsize firm. Like many professions, engineering has historically been a male-dominated field, but that is rapidly changing. Mary Ellen has the potential to really grow with this organization.

For her interviews, Mary Ellen knew enough to "dress the part" in a business suit, but now that she is a part of the organization, its lack of an official dress code policy has left her at a loss as to what to wear every day. Most of the men in the office wear a polo shirt and khaki pants. There are currently no women in senior management, so Mary Ellen has no role models on appropriate attire. Since dress is clearly not a priority to the organization, she assumes it does not matter to her success there. She typically wears her college look to work: casual pants, youthful tops, tousled hair, and large, dangling earrings.

After a few months on the job, Mary Ellen starts going to clients' offices to consult on projects and present proposals for new jobs. She never considered that although her appearance was apparently OK at the office, clients might get a different impression. Although her firm had the most competitive bid on a project several times in a row, it did not get the work. After the third lost piece of business, the head of the firm called a trusted client and asked why the firm had not gotten the job. The client said, "It's hard to put my finger on it exactly, but we just did not have faith that Mary Ellen could really handle this job."

As a consequence, management stopped sending Mary Ellen out to meet clients, thus keeping her in more of a support role to her peers. Meanwhile, her peers gained valuable time interfacing with clients and company owners; they quickly advanced and left Mary Ellen behind. Mary Ellen soon lost confidence in her abilities and wondered how her career got so off-track when she had thought this firm held such promise for her.

How big a part did Mary Ellen's unprofessional attire play in clients' lack of faith in her?

Where did the company err?

Where did Mary Ellen err, and what should she do now?

What lessons can you apply?

For our responses to these questions, visit our website, www.peggynoestevens.com.

SKILL #6
MANAGING YOUR PERSONAL LIFE

Now that we have explored in greater depth the effects of personal grooming on your brand, and we have expanded our discussion of your appearance to include your clothing as well, we will take up a related issue: how to manage your personal life.

The impact of your personal life on your career and your brand cannot be overestimated. So many people I work with feel out of control, as though they are not in charge but rather being carried down a swift stream, just floating along helplessly. When you experience this out-of-sorts feeling between work and personal life, it is just the time to call a "time-out" and reflect on the circumstances that led to that feeling.

At many times during my career, I have had difficulty dealing with an individual, and yet I could not for the life of me figure out what the trouble was. When I would discuss the situation with my boss and ask for guidance, I would sometimes hear the following: *So-and-so is going through a really tough time at home.* While of course I am sympathetic to home-based challenges (we all have our trials and tribulations), this still does not give someone license to treat others poorly. Furthermore, if I hadn't received the boss's insight about these personal problems, I would have just attached my own label to the employee's personal brand: DIFFICULT TO DEAL WITH.

It is very hard to separate the personal from the professional because we spend so much of our lives at work, but it is crucial that you take a step back and try to think objectively. Ask yourself what is creeping into your work life and affecting your day-to-day performance. Are you distracted at work because your family interrupts your day, causing you to lose your concentration? Are you late to work because of things you need to do for your family? Do you fail to attend events because of family obligations? Are you always running two steps behind, trying to keep up with your personal to-do list?

I am certainly not advising you to step away from your family in favor of work. I am merely encouraging you to talk to your family about your work obligations and how your family can help you achieve better synergy. I use the word *synergy* as opposed to *balance* because in my opinion, there is no such thing as work/life balance. You can't have true balance, but you can bring some synergy back to your life for what I call "work/life purpose." Everything should have a purpose in your life, and if it doesn't, why are you doing it? This skill explains how to identify that purpose and create a strategy for success in both your work and your family life. It will help you alleviate some stress and develop the synergy you need to solidify your brand.

You probably spend a great deal of time planning for others, whether it be for people in your family, strategies for your company, or community organizations or sports teams. When it comes to yourself, however, how often do you really take a look at how you are spending your time? It's easy to get muddled in day-to-day tactics and overwhelmed with responsibilities that prevent you from taking charge of your life. As you will learn here, taking a helicopter view of your life will help you begin to understand the components that make up your work/life purpose. When you discover how to manage your personal life with your brand in mind, you will be on the road to accomplishing all that you wish to accomplish in life.

DEVELOP A PERSONAL STRATEGY

Great marketers build plans, pure and simple. They focus on the strategy first and engage the tactics later. Writing down your personal strategy will help you determine how to build and market your most important product: your personal brand.

Becoming your own life strategist is essential to empowering yourself and energizing your career. Over the years, I have developed a process for creating a personal strategy that will allow you to create work/life synergy and thus improve your personal brand. The first step is to gain perspective by carving out some time each week to focus on your personal vision, whether it is on a weekend or during the week. Find someplace quiet where you can think, and take an introspective approach to your life.

I have listened to countless employees complain about their workload and the hours they put on the clock, but what do they reply when I ask, "What are you doing about it?" Most of them admit that rather than attempt to reduce their workload or better manage their time, they are doing nothing to resolve the issue. Remember, only you can take charge of your career; no one will do this for you. There were many times in my career as a manager that an employee was working very hard, so I just kept going along, thinking that things were great. I did not know the person was feeling frustrated until finally I could see it in his or her gestures and attitude, or I heard it from another employee. People can't fix something if they do not know that it's broken.

Stop and define the areas of your life that are either draining you or leaving you unfulfilled. Only you can understand the feeling you have when you look at your life from a helicopter view. This view can be achieved by conducting a gap analysis between your work life and your personal life, as demonstrated in the next section.

Work/Life Purpose Gap Analysis

In Figure 9 you see two pie charts with a list of different categories in a person's life. The pie chart on the left is an example of how a person might divide their pie to reflect time spent on each listed item. Study carefully how you use your time currently: What gets the lion's share of your attention? What areas of your life get less attention? Now fill in the blank chart on the right by allotting a slice of the pie for the amount of time you dedicate to each of these categories. (Feel free to add other categories that relate to your life.)

Once you have an understanding of these elements, ask yourself, *How do I wish to spend my time? What does winning look like?* It is unlikely that the pie chart you have filled out will match your aspirations—and this will allow you to figure out where the gaps are in your life. This is an analysis of the gaps in your work/life purpose. Who or what is draining you, and why? Why are you not able to accomplish more in your areas of interest? Where do you wish to spend your time?

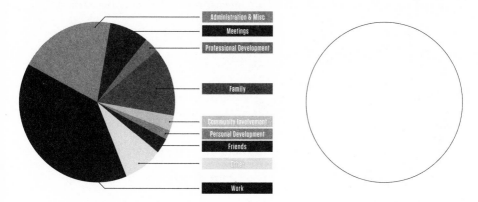

Figure 9: Work-life Analysis

Closing the Gaps

When you have finished the work/life purpose gap analysis, you must determine how to fill in those gaps. Do you need more help with tasks at home? Do you need to talk with your boss about workload, or let go of a few organizations or boards that you are a part of? This is your decision to make as part of your personal strategy, and it will require figuring out how you can spend more time in certain areas and less time in others. While you are making this determination, remember that you can't lie to yourself. You are the only person who knows how you feel about your life.

The following techniques will help you achieve your goals of spending more time in certain areas.

Set boundaries

Decide how deeply you need to be involved in certain areas of your life, and set those in your mind as standards to live by. This is particularly true in your personal life. Don't feel guilty if you need to bow out of a committee or a board or any other organization that has become tedious or overwhelming.

Manage expectations

Whether you are the employee or the manager, it is important to define your expectations of yourself. Is the amount of work you do allowing you to maintain synergy in your life? If not, what can you do to convey your boundaries to your boss and/or your staff? Where do you need help?

Nine times out of ten, the employee never asks for help. It's OK to do so, but make sure it is in a professional manner. Outline your workload, the areas of concern, and potential solutions to the problem. Work with your boss to determine priorities and expectations. If they are not laid out for you already, they need to be—or else you are walking a path with no directional signs. If you need to align yourself to create a better relationship with your boss and peers, make that effort.

Delegate to others

Do you rely on people to help you, or do you need to do everything by yourself? If you are a perfectionist or a micromanager, it's time to make a change. Is there a group of parents that you can pull together to carpool? Could you hire an intern who is willing to work for college credit and could take on your more tedious tasks? Is there another department in your company that should be helping you do a task? Help is all around you—just ask.

Build a strong network

Work on building a ladder of reliable people above and below your level. These individuals will help you navigate through your career; they can give you valuable suggestions on what they did to help themselves and how they go about managing their time.

Use career diagnostic tools

Sometimes we need help understanding ourselves and the roads we choose. Have you ever lifted your nose from the grindstone and asked yourself, *How did I get here? Why am I in this situation?* I encourage the use of traditional HR tools, such as 360s (interviews conducted with peers, supervisors, and employees) and PIs (predictive indexes) to better understand your personality and how others perceive you. Be fearless when asking for feedback; it is the very tool that can help you develop as a professional.

Expand your knowledge base

Become ferocious in your appetite for knowledge. Read books on leadership to gain an understanding of the styles of leadership-based success. Expanding your knowledge will help you correct your mistakes, enhance your strengths, and portray yourself as the person you aspire to become.

✦ ✦ ✦

Business, at the end of the day, comes down to metrics—the measurement of your accomplishments. Treat yourself as you treat your business;

determine what really works for you, and go with it. The work/life purpose gap analysis highlights the specific areas where you need to work on improvement. Use the tips for closing these gaps between your personal and professional lives to build your personal strategy. The strategy will in turn help you build your brand. When you have built the framework of your personal plan, set a timeline and keep yourself accountable to it. Use your strategy to do whatever needs to be done to truly build on your success both inside and outside of the office.

Like life itself, business is not without trials and tribulations, peaks and valleys, ebb and flow. Knowing where you are in your career life cycle—and where you want to be—keeps you in charge of the situation.

WORK/LIFE ETIQUETTE

In today's fast-paced business environment, because of the time you spend at your job, you can't avoid work overlapping with your personal life. Below are some points to remember—things that you may not always think about but that do contribute to the perception of your brand.

Pets

How do pets enter into the picture? Long-haired animals shed and leave unwanted hair on clothing and in your car. Keep a lint roller for such occasions, so that others are not affected by the shedding.

Also, remember that while you love your pet, others may not. If you are expecting guests in your home, be mindful of their comfort. Although it may not bother an animal lover when cats climb and jump on the kitchen countertops, this can be a turnoff for a colleague joining you for dinner at home.

Keep your pets in a closed-off area until you know whether your guests will be comfortable around them. I will never forget visiting one executive in his home office—his very exuberant border collie was fascinated with my white suit. The more the dog jumped up on me (uninvited, of course), the darker my suit became. Although my client instructed the dog to stop over and over, it was not until the fifth jump (and the need for one dry cleaning later) that he actually put the dog away! Needless to say, one of the first things I pointed out to the executive was the necessity of considering how others might feel about pets.

Family

No one knows better than I do about the daily juggle of working and children. Ask yourself, however, how often your workday is interrupted by your kids or your spouse or significant other calling you about day-to-day logistics and events. You may need to draw some clear boundaries and create an understanding with your family as to the best times to reach you during the workday.

Always be careful not to accept personal calls, unless it is an emergency, when you are in a meeting or are in the presence of others. If you need to take the call, then step outside to have the conversation, so as not to interrupt the meeting. Whether you are in the middle of an important business conversation or just discussing a minor office issue, don't annoy your colleagues by accepting a call from your spouse about dinner plans for the evening. Handle household issues before work or when you take a break in a private setting to avoid forcing people to wait for your attention at work.

Spouses

As an event planner, I conducted hundreds of social events and conventions where spouses were included in the mix. It always amazed me when the spouse would complain about the menu, the decor, the dress code, and such, as if he/she were leading the event. I have even seen spouses complain to a manager about how their wives or husbands are working too many hours. You can imagine the response from the boss who receives these complaints! Spouses are invited guests who should be gracious in every way to the host of the event and to any work colleagues who are present. If necessary, speak to your spouse or significant other about what you expect. You don't want his/her behavior to leave a long-term negative impression.

On the other hand, I have also seen spouses who have helped to propel their wife or husband's career by becoming an asset at work-related events. By being socially savvy, so he/she is wanted and even requested at events, a spouse can add to your personal brand in many subliminal ways.

✦ ✦ ✦

From taking an hour a week to develop your strategic plan to removing dog hair from the front seat of your car, what you do in your personal life plays an important part in the creation of your personal brand. When you learn how to use elements of your personal life to build your brand, you will discover the work/life synergy that is so essential to the professional presence.

PRO SCENARIO: MANAGING YOUR PERSONAL LIFE

Matt, a thirty-two-year-old account manager at a large advertising agency, is married with two small children. His wife, a schoolteacher, has been able to manage most of the things at home thus far, including shuttling kids to after-school activities, doing the grocery shopping, cleaning the house, and so forth. This has allowed Matt to focus almost entirely on work. This freedom has even allowed him to become the "go-to" guy for last-minute projects, client entertaining, and out-of-town trips.

Now, in order to advance her career, Matt's wife has gone back to school to get her master's degree. She can no longer do the majority of the "home management" tasks, and more and more of them are falling to Matt.

Matt quickly finds himself utterly overwhelmed with trying to meet the demands of his career, his home life, his volunteer commitments, and his personal hobbies. He is starting to feel that every one of these areas is being shortchanged, but rather than appreciate how to take a step back and evaluate his new situation, he keeps trying to juggle everything.

Not knowing the situation, his boss becomes suspicious when all of a sudden Matt is leaving the office in a rush at 5:00 p.m. rather than staying well into the evening, as had become his standard. He even declined an invitation to a recent weekend golf outing with clients! Matt's boss, suspicious by nature anyway, begins to wonder, *Is he preparing to leave the agency? If so, can we trust him with our most critical accounts?*

Rather than speaking to Matt, his boss reorganizes the account assignments and leaves Matt with the least desirable projects. In a panic, Matt goes to his boss for an explanation. After a heated conversation, they finally realize what is going on. Matt commits to taking the weekend to come up with a plan.

In the end, he steps down from two of the four volunteer boards he was sitting on, staying on only the ones he feels truly passionate about. He connects online with a parent carpool co-op that can take the kids to a couple of their after-school programs each week. This allows Matt to block one night a week and one weekend a month to work on projects and client entertaining. When possible, he entertains clients by taking them sailing, a personal hobby for which he no longer has much time on his own.

While Matt is unable to devote the excessive amount of time he used to give to work, his plan shows his boss that he is still committed to the organization. Because he no longer has the luxury of always being able to operate in last-minute mode, he has become more efficient during regular office hours and has learned to plan further ahead. In the end, he actually has become much more effective and strategic in all facets of his life.

What did Matt do wrong?

What did the agency do wrong?

How did they both turn things around?

What lessons can you apply?

For my responses to these questions, visit my website, www.peggynoestevens.com.

PART II
Summary

Although we seldom take time for ourselves in today's fast-paced business environment, to create a strong brand you must set aside a few moments for considering your personal strategy. This valuable block of time should become part of your monthly calendar. Creating a habit of giving yourself some "me" time will enable you to stop and review where you are in regard to your objectives and goals and how to achieve them.

Think of it like a business: No one can execute a successful strategy without monthly, quarterly, or annual reviews. This allows you to adjust and readjust needs, priorities, and tactics to get you where you need to go. At times you may feel overwhelmed with the detail involved, but eat the elephant one bite at a time. Once you realize that everything you put into this strategy is about you, you will understand that accomplishing your goals is the highest return on investment (ROI) that you can give yourself. It takes time and patience. Over time, as you make adjustments to really bring out your style, whether these involve your wardrobe or grooming or organizational skills, people will notice these positive changes.

Build your personal road map for the future, and you will begin taking charge of your career and your life. You will see how your personal life can be a key building block for your personal brand.

PART III: PROFESSIONAL

Put your game face on today—you can throw up

later when no one else is around.

OVERVIEW

When you are in a business environment, your brand depends not only on your knowledge of protocol and your personal skills but also on your professional skills.

Your professional interactions with co-workers affect your personal brand. One of the most important of these is formal interaction: the presentation. It could be a speech before an audience or a one-on-one meeting—no matter how many people are listening to your presentation or where it takes place, as long as you hold the floor, you are presenting your brand. As I introduce my own presentation to clients on personal brand, often during the first twenty minutes I pause quite purposefully, as if to make the room wonder, *What is she doing?* I then suggest that by now the audience has formed an impression of me, based on my professional presence.

"And how am I doing?" I ask, because we do evaluate the presenter, regardless of the content of a presentation. So the first skill in this section is about supporting your content with a positive image—and there you will find whatever advantages I can give you. Presentation techniques will also come in handy when attempting to master the other skill addressed in this part: how to run an effective meeting. As you learn about making these interactions successful, you'll begin thinking more about professional skills. How much should you share with your colleagues about your personal life? How much should you talk about other workers? Where do the lines between social and business interactions begin to blur, and how can you redefine them? Part III addresses these issues and lists actions as it describes the following skills:

Skill #7: Making Presentations

Skill #8: Running Effective Meetings

SKILL #7
MAKING PRESENTATIONS

The overhead lights turn off—the spotlight is on you. Whether you are talking one-on-one with a colleague or giving a speech in front of a room full of people, how you make a presentation can make or break your career. When you create applause by focusing the energy in the room around your message, you will command an elite airspace, a zone of influence that lasts. When, through self-promotion or lack of preparation, you make yourself more important than the message, the results can be deadly. And you can always sense when someone is on life support during a presentation that is spiraling downward.

One director at a major media company had earned quite a reputation for the dazzling, humorous presentations he would cook up for every sales meeting. These included a financial report about his publishing program woven in with music, movie, and pop culture references, along with witty lines about co-workers and himself, and comical but obvious plugs for his boss. The director did this successfully for a few years, pushing the envelope slightly in terms of length and taste.

At the culmination of one presentation, he prepared a slide that drew on a quip from a popular movie and called for his boss to be promoted to president of his division, a promotion everyone knew the boss was gunning for. What lent this moment an edge was that his boss's boss, a director of the firm and the man who would make the final decision, was sitting in the front row.

As word of this director's presentations spread, they became an "event" at each sales conference. Each presentation seemed to bring in a bigger audience—and take a few more risks with humor. It was obvious that a few of the director's peers began to resent, just a little, how much attention he received. What's more, it became harder each time to glean the business information from his jokes, movie lines, and wisecracks.

At last came an annual meeting, and the man and the presentation became bigger than the brand and the business. Our presenter emptied the kitchen sink into his multimedia presentation—graphics, film clips, music, jokes, and, amid all the sizzle, an update on his division. But he had taken the bridge too far. Caught up in his reputation, he'd assembled a half-hour presentation when his peers had been limited to ten minutes. The presentation was too garbled and complex to follow. He used a joke at the expense of someone who had been fired from the company, and included a film clip showing a topless actress. He bombed. While he didn't lose his job, he could have. His presentations from then forward were short and plain vanilla.

I once watched a high-potential employee give a presentation. He was rumored to be a future executive and was quickly moving up the ladder. This presentation took place at a national meeting before four hundred people. But the employee had never spoken in front of an audience of that size. He quickly lost his nerve; he stumbled, fumbled, and rambled to the point that you could feel the pain for him. It was as though a damp fog had drifted into the room. Needless to say, his poor performance derailed his personal brand. It was almost like turning off a light: one minute he was enjoying his potential, and the next he was worrying about his brand recovery.

Ah, corporate life! There are always ups and downs, ebb and flow. It is how you recover from the downs that is important. Skillful presentations can help you make sure *your* career has more flow than ebb.

THE FOUR GOALS OF EVERY SPEECH

To become a successful speaker, you need to have your goals in mind, just as when you are building your personal brand. These include not only the goals specific to your content but also the four main goals of any speech: to engage attention, to establish credibility, to deliver a message with impact, and to ensure that information is retained. In order to achieve these goals, you must have good content, good preparation, a good start, along with confidence and credibility.

The following discussion will teach you some of the most powerful techniques you will need to ensure that your speech is successful.

Goal 1: Engage Attention

It intrigues me that I am able to bring a room of two hundred people to full attention by just using two simple words: *bourbon tasting.* I am a former master bourbon taster, and I conducted tastings globally for years. I have been speaking publicly for more than twenty years now, on various topics, but it is my bourbon experience that taught me the most valuable lesson in how to capture attention. The topic of bourbon is different and unexpected during a business presentation. It piques your curiosity, leaving you wondering, *How does this fit with what she is about to say?* So I can feel the audience engaged to learn more.

A typical audience sits and waits for the speaker to appear, or at least for the person who introduces the speaker. You might even see an image over the stage or have a flier in hand—a snapshot of the person and a few words about what he or she does for a living, to set the stage for what you are about to hear. You don't always need a formal introduction, but having a third party to introduce you and explain your background or the purpose of the presentation can lend credibility—and can provide you with an opening so you don't have to jump in cold.

A popular suggestion from the experts is to open a speech with an attention grabber. This advice can be misleading, and some might understand it to mean sharing a joke, an off-topic story, a story about yourself, or a gimmick. Rather than *attention grabbing,* I prefer the word *engaging.* Some audiences, particularly in conference and workshop settings, are primed to learn, listen, and distill insights. Engage them! Instead of a pointless gimmick or a questionable joke, deliver an experience or an interactive moment that orients them to the work at hand.

I am a firm believer that every presentation is a story to be told. There is always a beginning, a middle, and an end. Thinking back to your childhood, do you remember how engaged you were when a story was read to you at bedtime or by a teacher at school? You and any other children around hung on every word, waiting for the next big move from the main character. Adult audiences are no different. They want a good story. They want to be entertained, to be touched emotionally through your actions and words. They want to be led to an affirmation of your credibility and persuaded to go your way. As we review in-depth techniques for building your professional platform, keep in mind this question: *What is the story?*

Open your presentation by engaging the audience immediately in the following ways.

Focus on the lesson

Most important, decide early on, *What is my takeaway? What is the top message that I want everyone in the room to leave with today?* Focus on this message as you develop your script. I use the word *script* intentionally, because I believe that presenting is a form of theater. You are on stage, delivering a scripted message—and praying for applause at the end! This message should be a beacon for the audience to recognize and follow throughout your speech.

Start with a detail to focus on

Coordinate with your leadoff person to introduce you briefly, taking just a few seconds. Then, start your talk with a detail that is unique, beyond expectations. Use stories, music references, local information, and surprising statistics—what I like to call the "flypaper" that pulls the audience in, so they can follow you to the next piece.

Create an elevator pitch

I challenge the people I coach to write their own bio and read it back to me while I listen for that "wow" factor. Building your brand requires you to hone a statement about yourself, including an "elevator pitch" of who you are and what you can do—brief and to the point, as if you could express it to an executive you meet on a short elevator ride. Develop a symbolic story—like mine based on bourbon tasting—that people associate with you as a person or industry professional. Use this story in your presentation and throughout your efforts at personal branding.

Avoid the gender trap

Women should avoid the common trap of breaking the ice with stories about their kids and families. Men should avoid recycling sports anecdotes or tales from the golf course. You have little to gain by underscoring the gender typing that most of us do (even if it is unconscious).

Be candid

Say something revealing about yourself, but make sure that it's relevant. It may be something about your current job, a unique and positive experience you've had, or an aspiration you desire to reach through the material you plan to cover. By sharing your vision, as long as it pertains to the topic at hand, you express sincerity to your audience and encourage them to trust you.

Goal 2: Establish Credibility

The cornerstone of a successful speech or presentation is simple: Know your audience and their concerns. Most presentations that fail do so because the speaker did not take the time to find out enough about his/her audience. Knowing your audience means seeking as much information as possible in advance so that you can successfully match your message to their interests and needs. The following techniques will help you achieve this important goal.

Provide background

Portray your background in a few sentences to preemptively answer *why* you are speaking. This is especially necessary if the audience does not know you personally. If it is an internal meeting, then you may forgo the background and focus on why you are poised to present this topic: "As director of marketing, I hope to give you a vision of the future advertising campaign . . ."

Do your homework

Demonstrate your sincerity by knowing your audience. This is essential—I will say this again, *essential*—to a successful presentation. Knowing the temperament, culture, background, gender, demographics, and psychographics of an audience will direct your material and conversation, because you will need to tee up the takeaway message to fit each group. In other words, delivering a heavy financial presentation to a nonfinancial audience will cause their eyes to glaze over; knowing this audience, you would break down your charts, simplify, and build in time for feedback, questions, and interaction. On the flip side, an executive audience would want the high-level, high-profile financial analysis that they can sink their teeth into. Truly understanding your content and having backup research or facts to support your message is necessary for a clean delivery.

Avoid negativity

Even when you think you know the audience, they can still surprise you with their reaction to the information. No one has a crystal ball that shows how an audience will react; even some of the best Broadway shows and comedians fall short. When the news is bad, try to maintain a positive outlook. The toughest presentations involve giving information that people do not want to hear, but the power of your intention will aid you. Include a follow-up discussion afterward to gain feedback from the attendees; asking them to guide you on your next steps can help you persuade them to buy in to your message. You will not always hit a home run, but when you need a triple and hit only a single, follow-up feedback will also guide you on your next time up to bat.

I gave a high-profile strategy presentation to a third party from whom my client needed buy-in. I knew several of the folks in the room from past business together and had excellent relationships with them. The main decision maker to whom I was really presenting was not going to like what I had to say, so I needed to be cautious yet firm. The net results: After the meeting, several people came up to me and commented on what a great style I had used in delivering the message. The content was clear and the tone professional, they told me. The one person I needed to "turn around," however, was ready to bite steel. He insinuated to others that I had come across negatively.

Hmmm—two totally different analyses of the same event. Who was right? It was a big pill to swallow, because I knew that creating a negative reaction was *not* my intention . . . but I had to ask myself, *What could I have done differently?* For some folks, nothing. But for the audience that mattered most in this case, the presentation had fallen short. I went to great lengths afterward, with follow-up meetings and phone calls, to break down the information into a more accessible format. Sometimes people just need to have time to digest and ask questions, and you do not always have that luxury during a scheduled time. It truly worked in this case, though; after slowing down the parts and pieces through follow-up gestures, we came to a fruitful conclusion. The point is, I stayed focused on the desired outcome and changed my approach to fit the needs of the client.

Goal 3: Deliver a Message with Impact

Just as a good story has a central theme, so too does your presentation need to have a central message. Your entire presentation should focus on delivering this message in as engaging a manner as possible. The following techniques will help you accomplish this goal.

Use visual images and metaphors

Let's face it: Words on a PowerPoint slide can be extremely boring. Using the right graphics and layout and giving careful attention to keeping the message clear can help you sell the ideas. But while visually rich content is desirable, too many bells and whistles can overstimulate the audience and drown the message, as well as introduce technological issues. Balance is key when using visuals during a presentation; add a degree of interest or drive home a point by personifying your words with a picture.

Use examples

Storytelling again comes to the rescue. Notice how I have used examples throughout this book to support the lessons from my training and the direction I want to take. Real-life examples mean just that: from real life. They offer something relevant to the audience and paint a picture in their minds, which can help them grasp concepts—and remember them.

Use signposts

Phrases like *My point is this* and *The most important thing to remember is* act as signs that point to important concepts. You also could number your points, as in, *I'll be offering* three *ideas—the* first *one is* . . . Some speech trainers call these "transitions." Let's go back to the idea of storytelling: You have to slow down and emphasize certain parts of the story in order to build momentum. Break down a tricky area in a way the audience can understand, or tell them straight out what is going to happen next by outlining objectives or providing agendas they can follow.

Goal 4: Ensure That Information Is Retained

Once you have communicated your message to your audience, you must make sure that they retain the information after your presentation is over. Many presenters stumble over this aspect of public speaking, but it does not have to be difficult. A few simple techniques will help ensure that your message sticks.

Ask the audience

This technique is simple and straightforward—just ask. I purposely stop at certain times during my presentation, whether it is to a crowd or in a one-on-one meeting, and ask, "Are you with me? Is this clear to you? Have I confused you? What more can I explain?" Sometimes the audience will just nod their heads *yes* in an attempt to move on, but don't forget to read their faces: Are they perplexed? Does it look as though they are processing the information? Have they remained a little too quiet after your question? Don't continue to unload new information on them unless you know where they stand. You must be fearless about the feedback and thank them for any questions they have shared, no matter how emotional, basic, or controversial they might be. Good presenters know their stuff and anticipate their audience's questions as best they can.

Slow down

Ease your pace as you transition to your closing. Use a statement like "Let me pause for questions while we think about the board's plan of action for next year." Or, "Please take a moment to review the next steps, and then let's take some time to discuss."

Memorize your closing

Review your main points and encourage people to write them down. Better yet, provide a handout that boils the presentation down to your main points. This will ensure that your takeaway message delivers an impact on your audience. Use phrases to tip them off that you are nearing the finish line, such as "To conclude, I want to thank you for your time and attention, and ask that you keep in mind . . ."

Motivate the audience

For your presentation to be meaningful, you must ask your listeners to take an action, ask a question, have an emotional response, or think differently in some way. Make it clear what you're asking them to do—and if you don't know, rethink the purpose of your speech. All great salespeople ask for the order in the end, and you need to do so as well. Circle back to your opening and the key takeaway you identified as the beacon to follow.

Have you ever sat through a presentation only to leave scratching your head, thinking, *What were they trying to say?* Or worse, *That was a waste of time.* This is the result you face when the message content is not clear. Even when you speak out during a one-on-one meeting, remember to ask yourself, *What is the goal?* and *What are the takeaways?* Stay focused on your intent, and make sure that by the end of your presentation, it becomes the audience's intent, too.

GUIDELINES FOR PRESENTATION AND DELIVERY

Once you have your goals in mind, use the following guidelines to achieve them by delivering a strong presentation. As you read through them, think about your own presentation style and what you can do to improve it. The techniques may seem simple, but they are absolutely essential for building your personal brand.

Gestures

Controlled gestures are of the utmost importance. Arms and hands must be fluid; if movements are choppy or there is no flow, it can be jarring or distracting. Your gestures should match your words. For example, if you're stating that sales are higher, then your hand gesture should signal this as well (raise your hand, don't lower it). As we discussed in part I, your posture will play a huge role in giving the impression of confidence. Slouch, and you look defeated; stand upright with an open chest, and you might look invincible.

Diplomacy

How do you deliver bad or difficult news without losing focus on the end result? How you tee up an issue, carefully choosing the words to wrap it in, can mean the difference between attentive listeners and an angry mob. Sometimes you can deliver a message on a feather and people still will be turned off, but the bottom line is always that your intentions are sincere. Letting people know where you stand and voicing your stance clearly will bring transparency to your message.

Vocal Quality

Speaking slowly and clearly will aid in your delivery. Some presenters are so soft-spoken or so nauseatingly loud that you can't engage in the message; instead, you detour into what I call "struggled listening." When your audience is constantly thinking, *I can't hear you!* (or worse, *You're taking all the air out of the room!*) their ability to pay attention deteriorates. As we discussed earlier, always speak from the diaphragm, using breath support.

I recently coached a woman who was a working mother and always felt rushed—two steps behind, trying to fit ten pounds of sugar in a five-pound bag. Her life was filled to overflowing, and even though I was coaching her on work/life purpose and organization skills, I felt it necessary to spend time on her rushed speech, flailing arms, and high-pitched, almost whiny voice. It made sense to me when her manager told me she always appeared out of control and emotional; her voice and gestures did much to support this perception. I told my client that she needed to pause and breathe at the end of each sentence, because the energy it took to listen to her was actually causing me to be edgy and agitated. People rub off on one another, and when you spend time with someone it is hard to avoid absorbing his/her energy and demeanor. While this woman was a very competent professional and a true workhorse, her demeanor was hindering her performance. All we needed to do was slow her speech, not her working pace or her workload.

Quality Materials

Always be prepared when attending a presentation; consider what you might need well in advance, and make sure you'll have it handy when the time comes. Carry a portfolio with paper and a pen for taking notes, even if you are conducting the presentation; the portfolio should be of quality material, and take a professional pen to take notes. If auxiliary pieces such as a laser pointer or a remote control help you, then by all means, purchase them. Do a mental walk-through of how you use these materials, so as not to fumble with them. You want to appear polished and your presentation to be fluid.

Follow-up

You gave the presentation your all. Now find out the audience's reaction: Where did you land? After any presentation, leave ample room for questions. It is also a great idea to have a last slide that reads NEXT STEPS . . . and gives a sequence of how things could move forward. If the presentation was to several individuals, follow protocol by requesting feedback from the next level up (your superiors). If you are the host of the presentation, and if it is appropriate, send a note thanking the participants for their time and attention.

CONFIDENCE-BUILDING TECHNIQUES

Learning specific guidelines for speaking is essential, but they are useless if you do not have the confidence you need to deliver a presentation. Building a confident presentation style will increase your confidence in your own brand and communicate that sense to others, giving them confidence in your brand as well. The following are my recommendations for increasing your sense of self-reliance.

Control the Fear of Public Speaking

Have you ever seen someone pass out from public speaking? Probably not. Nonetheless, it is a scary idea to some and certainly can be a real phobia. Indeed, public speaking has remained one of the things that cause people the most stress, consistently appearing on the list of the top ten things people fear! I try very hard to change this outlook, however, by turning the model inside out and suggesting that public speaking can be one of the most rewarding, energizing, and impactful things you do in your life.

I will always say that a little bit of nerves is a good thing for getting your juices flowing—your adrenal glands, that is. Just ask any athlete! They know that 100 percent calm is not the desired state when you want to give a great performance. What you want is the feeling of being a thoroughbred ready to enter the gate before a race—that *I can't wait to get there* feeling. Tap into that internal power by mentally preparing yourself, visualizing the success of your speech. No, visualization is not my invention (I wish it were), but it does work!

My mantra when giving a speech is this: *Who are we?* Let me explain.

Something dawned on me early in my career; I credit my father, a master of diplomacy and winner of the gold medal in optimism. It is this: Everyone you ever have met or will meet is a daughter, a son, a sister, a brother, a mother, or a father. This is common ground we all share as humans, regardless of title, level, prestige, or position. When you begin thinking of the people you present to as just that—people—the professional presence message resonates. Why should you be fearful of people who are in the very same shoes as you?

I am sure that by now you are thinking, *Hey, my career is riding on this, and this book is supposed to be about being* better—*right?* Correct, but in this case recognizing our sameness is a positive and helpful step. And anyway, this book, and any training classes or private coaching, will never be able to give you the internal power you possess—the power to decide for yourself that fear and failure are just part of the game of life, and it is all OK. It's what helps us grow and become better. Or as Katharine Hepburn said, "Be yourself—it's a tough act to follow."

Don't Worry About Mistakes

According to Denis Waitley, "Failure is our teacher and not our undertaker." I think that beneath the fear of speaking is the thought, *Oh my God, I might fail.* Well, so what? What doesn't kill you makes you stronger. Laugh at your mistakes, learn from them, and move on. Give yourself the permission not to be perfect, and psych your psyche into being excited for the opportunity and ready for the challenge. Try living with the thought, *No one knows this material like I do.* That is why, of course, you were chosen as the presenter.

Take Charge of the Room

When you're "onstage," you are in charge, and the audience likes to know this. I always joke that when it comes to pilots and doctors, I prefer the confident ones! Of course, we all want someone in charge who seems as though he/she knows what to do. We always will lend an ear and listen to people who have something worthwhile to say and who believe in what they say.

As a speaker, when you feel as though the audience is overwhelming you or not quite paying attention, shift your body language as if to become a little larger. Raise your voice a little to get their attention, and then you can return to your original tone. I used to conduct tours at a bourbon distillery, and whenever a few stragglers veered from the group, I would hold my hand up and say, "Is everybody with me?" Asking a question requires a response, which should bring the attention back to you. The opposite sometimes works too, so try going silent for a lengthy pause; once your audience notices, their attention will refocus on you.

Listening for restlessness in the crowd is important, but you also want to prevent straying concentration in the first place. Set expectations and have a clear agenda for the meeting so participants know where they stand and where you are at all times. Taking charge of the room is about communicating with the audience. Explain your role clearly and they will do their part to follow. Always provide good, solid direction and facilitation, following the agenda so that people regard you as organized, efficient, and well informed.

Avoid Snipers in the Audience

Often there are people in the audience who are out to make things difficult, who want to create traps or pitfalls for you; I call these people "snipers." They're the ones who have no fear of spouting off negative challenges, and they're usually smiling like the Cheshire cat after they feel they have derailed you. My best advice is to remain unshaken—if not inwardly, then in your appearance, with your facial expression neutral and your body stance and posture confident and strong. Listen carefully to the sniper's question, then repeat it back for clarity; this gives you time to think of an answer. Then decide for yourself whether you have a good answer that will put the issue to bed or whether the question is going to set off a firestorm and derail you. If so, the best-case scenario is to thank the person for the question and say that you will table it until the end or after a break (so you can come up with an answer or even "forget" to address the issue), or suggest that he/she find you after the meeting to discuss it briefly. Blame it on time, lengthy agenda, or whatever—but let the sniper know you appreciate the question.

Stand Your Ground on Issues

There are times that postponing just won't do, however, and a person of greater authority or a difficult person wants an answer—and he/she wants it *now*. If this is the case, remember, your body language will show confidence—or defeat—in your answer, so choose the right stance and posture. Active listening is key here, because you need to break down the components of the question in order to answer fully. If you are in a disagreement, then say, "I am sorry you feel that way, but I respect your opinion. Is this something we may discuss further after the meeting?"

Use the One Thousand-Mile Stare

In the extreme case that a sniper goes over the top in an attempt to discredit you or even intimidate you while you are presenting, remember the animal theory. When an animal looks its enemy in the eye, it is ready to go toe to toe; the animal that looks away from an opponent usually walks away from the conflict in the end. So keep your eyes focused directly on the sniper, even if during a meeting you feel as though he/she is one thousand miles away, and this person will know you are not the least bit intimidated. Walk closer to the person if possible; as the presenter, more than likely you are standing, and you will appear bigger than you are. Walking forward also tells someone you are not fearful. Remember that bullies like to dominate and suck the air right out of the room. You can take charge of the situation—and it's up to you to do so.

Read the Audience

Get nonverbal feedback from the audience by using their physical expressions to help guide your presentation. I used to be surprised at times when I thought I gave a presentation that was so-so and yet received great feedback afterward. In these instances, I had not gotten a feel for the energy of the crowd during the presentation. I know how crucial it is to be cognizant of the way crowd members sit and their facial expressions. Are they nodding while you speak (in assurance), or shaking their head (to the contrary)? Are they restless, fidgeting in their chairs and looking at their watches? This all is part of the human read and should cue you as to when you need to take a break, spice things up, or call it quits.

✦ ✦ ✦

Presentations are just one of the professional interactions we have with people as we work to develop our brand. The professional presence demands that we also understand how to interact professionally with individuals in a meeting setting—and that is the topic of the next skill section.

PRO SCENARIO: MAKING PRESENTATIONS

Charlotte is a thirty-five-year-old PhD in the field of child psychology. She received her doctorate from a university on the West Coast, worked there for several years, and was highly respected in that region. She recently accepted a position with a large organization in Chicago, and while she has joined a couple of professional organizations, she is still establishing herself within her new community of professional peers.

Charlotte had planned to attend an annual regional convention for those in the field of child behavior, and she was excited about the opportunity to meet a lot of colleagues who also specialize in treating young children with autism. Two days before the conference, a co-worker who was to be a speaker there became very ill and asked Charlotte to step in for her. Although making presentations is not Charlotte's favorite thing to do, the speech was within her area of expertise and she was glad to help a colleague. She spent the next couple of days dusting off a presentation she had given at a similar conference in California. She practiced a few times and made the appropriate technical updates.

When the day arrived, Charlotte made her way to the convention room and gave herself sufficient time to test the microphone and projector, making sure she felt comfortable on the stage and was ready to go. When it was time for the presentation, there was no one in the room to introduce her, so she just got up, gave her name and explained that she was there to fill in for her colleague, and began her presentation. After she finished, Charlotte felt good about the material, her presentation style, and her delivery. She was surprised, however, that very few people raised questions during the Q&A session. In fact, the audience seemed disinterested, and hardly anyone remained afterward for further discussion, which is unusual for professionals in her field.

What did Charlotte do wrong? Think back to the four goals of giving a presentation. Did she remember them all?

Where did the conference organizer go wrong?

What lessons can you apply?

For my responses to these questions, visit my website, www.peggynoestevens.com.

SKILL #8
Running Effective Meetings

When trying to coach managers on how to plan meetings, most experts talk about the process of the meeting itself: taking notes, starting and ending on time, having an agenda. I prefer an approach that focuses on you, the meeting leader, and how you can develop the plan that makes meetings work best. Effective meetings are run by prepared leaders who invest the time to ensure that the team members who attend are informed, made comfortable, and given a meaningful role and a chance to contribute. A meeting doesn't just happen successfully; it must be run by you, or it will fail.

This is an area of particular interest to me, as I have developed a national reputation for excellence in meeting and event planning, and over the course of thousands of meetings, I have learned what is required to make an important meeting succeed for you. My clients often write me after our work together with thanks and praise for the positive impact these methods had on their business processes and meetings.

I will tell you, however, that I have also attended plenty of what I call "disaster meetings." Reflecting back, I know that the derailment always stemmed from a lack of respect for the other people in the room. This problem with meetings usually stems from taking things too personally or getting too emotionally involved—not respecting the professional goal and outcome of the meeting. Know the difference between passion and emotion. I praise passionate speakers and facilitators; it is the emotional employee who loses the attention of the audience. There is always going to be some subject matter that causes emotions to stir, and when emotions escalate, intelligence declines; it is important to balance this lack of order with the sensible suggestions below.

HOW TO RUN A SUCCESSFUL MEETING

Here are some do's and don'ts for running a successful meeting.

Choose Your Meetings Wisely

Evaluate whether the meeting is necessary at all. Could it be handled instead through an e-mail, a lunch date, or a conference call? Some corporations have policies that are intended to save their employees' energy and protect them from burnout, such as designating *No Friday meetings* or prohibiting meetings from ending later than 5:00 p.m. Don't meet just to punch the ticket. If you do not have a valid agenda, then the issue can be addressed by e-mail and phone.

Identify Your Objectives

"Meeting after exhausting meeting" is what I hear many of my clients say. They are "stuck" in all-day meetings, they complain, leaving them unable to complete their work. It seems sometimes that we meet just to meet and "check off a box." But the decision to hold a meeting should begin instead with a series of questions: What are the objectives? Can you accomplish this task through an e-mail that asks for a simple response on one issue? Can it be a quick conference call, so as not to waste the time of people who would otherwise have to travel to be present? By determining the objectives you wish to cover and the issues you hope to solve during this meeting, you might realize that in fact the meeting itself is unnecessary. Even if you find that it *is* necessary, now you have the beginnings of your agenda.

Identify Your Message

Once you have identified your objectives, you must determine what message you need to convey. What is the message you wish people to take away from the meeting—the information that you wish to have clearly conveyed? How should you deliver the content? Is it a powwow, where you need feedback from everyone, or a closed meeting, where you handle information that is sensitive? Thinking about your audience, which is so important when delivering a presentation, is also key to the delivery and tone you will set at the meeting.

Create an Effective Agenda

Give an introduction stating any objectives you have and the amount of time it will take to cover these objectives, so participants are aware of how much time and what direction the meeting should take. Think hard about the subject matter, and prioritize by tackling the toughest topics first, easing into smaller items. Think of the best flow for the meeting. Does one topic stem from another? Do you need to make a decision on a particular topic before you can move any further?

Identify Participants' Roles

Many times during meetings we look around the room and say, "Where is so-and-so? He/she really needed to participate in this." As the host of a meeting, you need to think carefully through the roles, backgrounds, and titles of key players to ensure that the meeting includes all the folks who need to be there. If you are unsure of someone's role, or of which person has a certain role in their department, just ask someone. Clarity on the front end of a meeting invitation will save a tremendous amount of time that would otherwise be devoted to backpedaling, trying to catch up with people who were missing.

Be mindful as well of the various titles and authority levels of those you invite to a meeting. Those with higher authority may not need to be involved in tactical issues but would rather see the final presentation and results. Use your judgment, but also communicate with your boss or an executive to identify what types of meetings should involve them. It's important to be clear about this so you are on the same page.

I had a client who acted on his own authority, setting meetings at any time without checking with participants, telling them that they just "needed to be there." This is an example of flexing your own muscle without consideration for anyone else. It was irritating and counterproductive to my client's colleagues; people began to resent the project—and moreover, him. Was it really such a hard thing to ask in advance about others' availability? Lack of courtesy and professional presence made the project a tedious one. After hearing enough chatter from participants, I simply addressed the situation with him. I relayed how, although I saw that he was frustrated when people couldn't attend, we all had the same goal of wanting to make the project succeed. It ended up being more work to backtrack and reschedule than to determine the calendar in advance, using a simple tool like Outlook calendars to solve the problem. He was receptive and began to use Outlook, thrilled with the capability to check the status of participants in advance. Simple problem, simple solution.

Be Ready for Surprises

Even if you are not the one creating the meeting agenda, you should know who is coming to the meeting. I have both attended and facilitated meetings where there was a "surprise guest" just to get participants in a lather. This person may be either at a higher level of authority or someone you just plain did not expect. Never act surprised when this happens; welcome the person, acknowledge that you are glad he/she could join you, and then move forward.

If you are attending a meeting and need to bring extra people for whatever reason, contact the host and let him/her know. Food may have been arranged and/or tables configured for the meeting with a certain number of people in mind. Never sabotage someone's meeting by changing the agenda or the participants when you are not the host. This has certainly happened to me. I requested a meeting once with an executive and listed who would be in the meeting and the topics we were there to discuss. When I showed up for the meeting, the executive came out to greet me and then proceeded to tell me how the meeting would go, contrary to original content. Without any regard for my mission in calling the meeting, he changed the agenda and force-fed the group a presentation on a totally different topic! The rest of the group was frustrated and confused; he had totally derailed the meeting and left us unable to address the original purpose. Hijacking a meeting in this way is not only tasteless, it also damages relationships and trust. This certainly can happen in business; it is best to redirect the conversation appropriately if you are in a position to do so.

Beware of "Drainers"

I have a name for people who act like the star of the show, who bog down a meeting by sending negative vibes and setting up roadblocks: "drainers." Look at it in the same way as going to someone's home for dinner; the host of the meeting is in charge of the meeting. Anticipate the drainers before the meeting; it may be in your best interest to meet with them first. By going over some topics in advance, you can manage their expectations.

Stars of the show need to let everyone know they are smartest or are in charge, even when they're not. Acknowledge their great participation, and then ask others for their view. Drainers tend to suffocate the other participants because they want everything to go their way. Keep the meeting flowing by asking others to chime in; gauge their thoughts and how they react to what the star says, and facilitate their participation.

Consider Assigning Seats

We are creatures of comfort, and so we choose to sit by people we like. Do what you can to shake up the seating arrangement for a more effective meeting with better results. When conducting strategy sessions or meetings, I strategically seat together participants who may not know each other in order to encourage dialogue. Break up troublemakers and thwart stars and drainers by seating them near people of authority.

Be Prepared

Ensure that multimedia equipment is set up, running in proper order, and ready to go before the meeting begins. For multiple presentations, ask presenters to use only one computer so setup and teardown times are minimal. Wasting time with technical delays is a major pet peeve of executives. Regardless of the technology to be used, ensure that you understand the layout of the room and where equipment will be placed. Do a test run so that by the time the very first person walks into the room, you are ready to go.

Technology is tricky. Things can and will go wrong. So what is the backup plan? Do you have hard copies of the presentation or program to give as a backup, just in case? As an event planner, I held my breath countless times, praying that the speakers at my conferences would sail through their presentations without malfunction. What allowed me to sleep at night were prior rehearsals and run-throughs, so I knew exactly what I was walking into the next day.

Inform Participants

Many times people attend a meeting to collect and exchange information. It is most helpful when you give participants the proverbial "heads-up" on the agenda, so they may come prepared. What information is available to you? Share what you can with the meeting's participants. It is also important to send out any detailed topic that requires prior knowledge in advance of the meeting. You will save a considerable amount of time because you can tackle the agenda topics right away, without losing ground by having to explain the backdrop of the agenda and the landscape of issues.

Control Your Time

The older I get, the more important time becomes, because jam-packed schedules and heavy workloads are a reality. Using your time effectively by actually accomplishing the agenda will encourage people to attend your meetings. I took part in a series of meetings where the facilitator promised that they would run only thirty minutes to an hour. Two hours later we were all in pain because the subject matter kept veering away and topics not on the agenda kept creeping up, diluting the original objectives—and that was just the first meeting. More and more, the people scheduled for those future meetings would decline and avoid them, knowing they would get trapped. You don't want people to dread your meetings.

Many boards of directors assign time limits to agenda topics to manage discussions and keep sidebar conversations from throwing a meeting off topic. When you're the host and it feels as though the discussion is veering away from the agenda, you and you alone are responsible for getting back on track with the issues. It is always wise to leave room for overage by building a fifteen- to thirty-minute cushion into the agenda. If you're lucky, you won't need the cushion and can actually end the meeting early, making everyone happy.

Appoint a Facilitator

Acknowledge the importance of time by appointing a facilitator to manage the course of the day in order to stay productive, especially if you are not savvy about juggling the agenda and time. A timekeeper for the meeting can help you monitor the agenda and stay on topic. Your company may have designated facilitators within the organization whom you can call on to help you.

Practice Active Listening

Active listening is essential no matter what content you are covering. After all, that is why you have a meeting: to communicate. When participants deliver a message in reply, read between the lines: Are they confused? Frustrated? Did they understand what you were trying to convey? Ask participants the key questions: *Does everyone understand? Are there any further issues to discuss?* For a meeting leader, the biggest disappointment is when everyone walks away nodding their heads *yes,* but you hear later that some attendees really feel differently. In your meetings, make sure *yes* and *no* mean just that.

I once conducted a meeting with high-level clientele from several industries. I left feeling elated by the response of the participants, who had accepted and applauded the ideas put before them, only to find out later that they backtracked on their commitment. They did not have the communication skills or the courage to address their concerns in an open and professional manner, and as the meeting leader, it was my job to make up for that by listening actively and questioning them thoroughly to be sure they understood. Always encourage candor; it is the only way to move forward. You may need to probe and pull out responses if the room is too quiet afterward; listen when you do have a response so you can address any issues.

Create a Culture of Respect

You can encourage mutual respect and professionalism in your meetings by sticking to your protocol and etiquette training. All voices should be heard in a meeting, and if the environment is overrun by bullies and intimidation, some of your brightest employees might not be heard. Monitor this type of problem, and identify who needs protocol coaching. Unfortunately, meetings can be a catalyst for emotion and disagreement. A former executive once reminded me that you can agree to disagree about some things—that's just business. But at some point you need to reach agreement on the important points. Tearing someone down or embarrassing a person to get your point heard is nothing more than schoolyard bullying. It deteriorates the intelligence of the whole. Remind meeting participants that one of us alone is not as smart as all of us together.

Save Space for "Parking"

I keep a "parking lot" list at any meeting I conduct, because issues will always come up that you don't anticipate. If it is appropriate to address these directly during the meeting, then by all means, do so. If an issue will take you on a different course and put the meeting off track, however, place it in the parking lot file for later. Acknowledge that the parking lot questions will be addressed at a later date, and then keep that promise or follow up with the individual who was concerned.

Plan on the Fly

Survey the crowd as the meeting progresses, reading facial expressions and body language. Take time during breaks to circle the room and ask people for feedback. Are they getting what they need from the meeting? Is there something that requires more attention? If so, change it on the fly. While your failure to stick to the agenda can seem as though you've misled participants, failing to adjust to the circumstances can convey rigidity and inability to change. Fast planning can mean the difference between a successful meeting and a bust.

Manage Expectations

When you set objectives for a meeting, you set goals but not always priorities. As a meeting heads toward the end, take a step back with all the information and think, *What are the net results?* Then prioritize with the group to lay out next steps that participants can act upon to show that the content of the meeting has been understood.

Summarize

After reviewing each participant's next steps and expectations for the group as a whole, summarize the meeting. Think in terms of the big picture: Where do you think you stand now? Was there anything the meeting did not cover that should be covered in the future? Taking a larger view shows that you care what people think about the content and the direction in which you are headed. An overview also might uncover any small leaks that need to be plugged.

The summary period is also a good time to ask participants whether they have any questions or comments. Remember, when people like what you have done in a meeting, they will usually come up to you afterward and say so. When everyone is silent and just walks out of the room upon conclusion, well . . . you just have to wonder.

✦ ✦ ✦

Now that you understand the basic skills needed to hold an effective meeting, let's spend a little time focusing on a particularly crucial type of meeting: the boardroom meeting.

BOARDROOM BASICS

Ah, the boardroom—where deals are sealed and careers can be shattered. If you want to get those promotions and move up through the management levels, sooner or later you will likely need to perform during a board of directors meeting or before some sort of senior management council. If you want better pay and greater responsibility, eventually you will need to present your views in a meeting held by top executives.

During my years as a corporate executive, I spent a tremendous amount of time sitting, presenting, negotiating, and creating in a boardroom. No one ever showed me a corporate meeting operations manual or a boardroom proclamation tacked to the wall, but I certainly watched and mirrored other executives and employees when learning the culture of the company and what I thought to be boardroom protocol. As I became more experienced, I began to understand that for effective management, process and style are foundational issues. It is easy to become frustrated with boardroom meetings, where the environment can be suffocating. Some of my clients complain to me about people raising their voices, shooting sarcastic comments, wasting valuable time on unessential conversation, and, frankly, not listening to one another. Meetings begin late and end late, with no formal objectives—they are a rudderless ship, if you will. If you have experienced anything like this in senior corporate meetings, then you know how quickly they can unravel and how participants can drop the business at hand, actually taking not a step forward but three steps back.

The following are boardroom basics that should help you avoid seeing your boardroom meeting derailed. This advice will get you started toward what all paths should eventually lead to—the need to conduct business.

Identify Your Company Policy

If your company doesn't have a policy for the boardroom, write one—or hire a protocol expert to write one. You may be surprised to find out that many companies lack any sort of protocol for conducting meetings. If that works for them, fine by me. But you just have to wonder what could be accomplished if there were some guidelines on form and function. Notice that I did not say *rules*—a term I avoid throughout this book because it is truly outdated. *Guidelines, culture creation,* and *professional presence* are more up my alley, and this is just what could be conveyed within your company. Talk to the administrative assistants, who instinctively know their bosses. They will be keenly aware of the likes and dislikes of those particular people; this way, you can avoid huge errors by understanding the best layout, design, and timing for your meetings when those individuals participate.

Presell Key Superiors

If possible, approach key colleagues and executives so that you can share with them the purpose, style, and length of your presentation, and get their buy-in. It sure is a confidence builder when you receive the "thumbs up" from an executive before going into a meeting. If you know he/she believes in your vision, you will ease into the rest of the presentation.

Stay Calm, Cool, and Collected

Most importantly (as I like to tell my clients), when trying to aspire to a bigger role, act as though you belong. So many employees walk into a boardroom situation with the "deer in headlights" syndrome, looking almost frozen—as if they were presenting to a firing squad. Remember, no matter how important the group, you have been invited as a guest for a reason: You know your material.

Your superiors are giving you a chance to be heard, so decide how you want them to hear you. Overconfidence shows arrogance, while being too humble and shy shows a lack of confidence. Meet yourself in the middle, and exude quiet, relaxed self-assuredness. Control your gestures by doing a self-check of your emotions before you enter the room, like a mental pep talk in the locker room before heading out to the big game. Give yourself some time to visualize your entrance and the reaction you wish to receive. Then make it happen.

 ## PRO SCENARIO: RUNNING EFFECTIVE MEETINGS

Brad is a hardworking young sales professional at a midsize manufacturing company. Although he has been with the organization for only a year, he just received a significant promotion to manage the sales effort for a brand-new product line. This came as a shock to many of the other salespeople who have been with the organization longer, and a couple of them are quite resentful that they now have to take direction from "the new kid."

To kick off the new promotion, Brad has been asked to organize a meeting of the entire team. He's nervous about it, but like everything else, he takes the challenge seriously and takes time to prepare.

Brad determines who the most critical meeting participants will be and reaches out to them to determine the best date and time. In his invitation, he clearly spells out the purpose of the meeting, a general agenda, and the role that each person is to play on the team.

On the day of the meeting he arrives early, makes sure the room is set up properly, and checks that the multimedia equipment is working. He also brings in refreshments—something that everyone appreciates but, he has noticed, often is overlooked at his company. When the first person arrives, Brad feels prepared and ready to go.

To his surprise, two of his colleagues, who had been passed over for his new role and were not on the launch team for this new product, show up to the meeting uninvited. Although this throws him, Brad keeps his cool and welcomes them. As the meeting begins, it becomes apparent that the two surprise guests have come hoping to see Brad stumble. However, they wind up seeing just the opposite. He keeps to his agenda, gives everyone the chance to participate, asks for feedback, and sets clear expectations and next steps for what is to happen after the kickoff. In the end, the two "drainers" actually wind up looking foolish, while Brad shines, making management all the more sure they have made the right promotion.

What did Brad do well?

What should management have done?

What lessons can you apply?

For my responses to these questions, visit my website, www.peggynoestevens.com.

PART III
SUMMARY

Delivering your message in a way that gives people the right impression is one of the most important and most difficult communication goals of personal branding. Confidence, fairness, and preparation are critical to giving a presentation or conducting a meeting while maintaining a professional aura. Be firm but open and willing to listen when running a meeting. By engaging listeners and establishing your credibility as you deliver a message with impact, you will ensure that information is retained. Avoid the disconnect that happens when the perceived message is not congruent with your intended and desired message. Say what you mean, and mean what you say—transparency, sincerity, and a commanding presence will accentuate your professionalism.

PART IV: PEOPLE

He would have a meltdown over his pencil lead breaking.

Can you imagine what he does when the big stuff happens?

OVERVIEW

Your personal brand depends not only on people's perception of you—how you act, how you appear, how you communicate—but also, and most important, on how you deal with people.

One area that has intrigued me throughout my career is the human read—trying to figure people out. For example, why didn't certain individuals like others, even though they had little interaction with them? How could I help my clients change a relationship when I had no idea what the relationship was to begin with? The amateur psychologist in me comes out when I begin to try to understand relationship dynamics.

People often come to me when they are experiencing conflict. When I coach others regarding their relationships with their peers, I may ask, "What is it about the other person that troubles you?"

The reply can range from an annoying personal habit or physical feature to a quibble over style to "I don't know—he/she just bugs me." Needless to say, when I peel back the layers on the vague answer, often I reveal that my client really has not thought deeply enough about what he or she could be doing to improve the relationship.

Often, we judge others without taking a look at ourselves first. Asking questions inwardly to encourage self-awareness can nip this in the bud: *Am I stirring the pot unnecessarily? Can I look beyond what's bothering me and find value in this person? Am I able to resolve the conflict and salvage the relationship? How would I wish to be approached if our roles in this situation were the reverse?*

This brings me to the explanation of why relationships are important: because when you build solid relationships with people, gain loyalty and trust, and exude likability, you become somewhat bulletproof to gossip and negative chatter from other influences. As we learned way back in Skill #3, people do business with people they like. A very wise boss once reminded me about the power of free will in saying that I could decide not to like anyone I was working with, but it was important that I make *them* like *me*! It was actually quite empowering.

Good counsel also came from a friend of mine when I was struggling with a particular employee and, frankly, had nothing good to say about the individual. My friend looked at me and said, "Even if all you can say about someone is that they have nice teeth, then do so. Find something, *anything*, positive and start building from there." And this is where I begin this final series of skills: putting a positive spin on dealing with people. Acknowledging that someone has value, no matter how big or small, is truly the foundation of professional presence. It is too Pollyanna to think that you won't encounter conflict with others, but always recognizing value in someone is the utmost sign of respect and will secure long-lasting relationships.

In *Driven: How Human Nature Shapes Our Choices,* by Paul Lawrence and Nitin Nohria (professors at Harvard Business School), the authors show

how biology and psychology inform how people act at work. The idea is that we are all influenced and guided by four drives: acquiring, bonding, learning, and defending. We work to obtain possessions and status *(acquire)*, develop close relationships with others *(bond)*, constantly seek information and new ideas *(learn)*, and aggressively protect what we perceive as ours *(defend)*. In the context of the workplace, this four-drive theory implies that every person, from the CEO to the most junior employee, will bring a predictable mind-set to work each day. All the other people engaged with the organization—customers, shareholders, creditors, suppliers, neighbors, regulators—share this mental framework. With this in mind, it should be clear that one-on-one engagement is particularly crucial to the drive for bonding and learning.

You don't have to read or agree with Lawrence and Nohria's book to acknowledge that in a workplace, you will either bond with others or you won't, depending on how you read the team. The skills in this part of the book are those you will need in order to manage people as you build your personal brand. In addition to being the most important, this is perhaps the most difficult of the four areas. After all, people are at the core of professional presence.

In this section, we will discuss the following skills:

Skill #9: Interacting with Colleagues

Skill #10: Knowing Your Team

Skill #11: Communicating with Transparency

Skill #12: Managing with Hospitality

Skill #13: Surviving a Performance Review

SKILL #9
INTERACTING WITH COLLEAGUES

To build your personal brand, it is essential that you follow the professional presence in your personal interactions with colleagues. You must be mindful of the dialogue you use when talking to peers, staff, and management. Are you pleasant? Preoccupied? Hurried? What sort of dialogue do you normally exchange with colleagues? Do you give people time with you? This chapter discusses how you can ensure positive and intentional interactions with your fellow employees.

PERSONAL INTERACTION TECHNIQUES

There are several things to consider when dealing with colleagues, but the underlying common denominator is to let them experience a consistent *you*. If every time they are around you, a different mood is revealed, your colleagues will find it difficult to relate to you. They may be apprehensive in approaching you, not knowing what to expect. Following these techniques can make you seem more approachable.

Avoid Negative Talk

Are you always positive? Or do you get caught up in complaining with peers in the trenches? When you are frustrated, sometimes it is necessary to work things out by bouncing them off another individual, but could this be to your detriment when he/she decides the information is worth repeating? Locker room communication can be a pitfall along your path of advancement. The wrong piece of information or negative talk in someone's hands can negate all the positive things you are trying to accomplish.

Respect Everyone

One story comes to mind about a peer who was not an organized individual and would blow people off when he thought that contact with them wasn't going to help his own career. He also had a knack for always coming back after damaging a relationship and then apologizing for his mistakes and how he had treated people. It was just like the tale of the boy who cried wolf; after a while I saw the pattern and became desensitized to the apologies. When he needed me and had something to gain, he sought me out for help. When I needed him, he wasn't there—and hence began the ritual of a one-sided relationship. Finally, after close to two years of this pattern, as we met and he was apologizing, I stopped him in midsentence.

"Why do you put yourself in the position of apologizing every time we meet?" I asked. "How about we try to get it right the first time, so we don't lose ground in our relationship?"

He seemed stunned, but I had discovered that it was necessary to set boundaries. People will always treat you how you allow them to treat you.

In developing your personal brand, you must set boundaries that require others to respect you, just as it is essential to respect others.

Set Boundaries

It is harder when you are dealing with someone of authority, but certain phrases—such as *What would you like to see me do?* and *How would you like us to communicate?*—are very helpful in establishing that first tier of boundaries. Have courage when seeking the best type of relationships available to you; you will recognize the ones you don't need. How? They are the ones you take home at night and wrestle to the ground, over and over. These relationships make you feel emotional and roadblocked instead of as if you're moving forward. You can't avoid poor relationships; as I like to say, even families fight. But you are truly in the company together, so you must find a way to resolve any issues.

If your experience with someone is extremely negative and this is affecting your health or mental state, it is time to involve your HR department. That is what they are there for—to create a distraction-free environment.

Manage Conflict

When it comes to this topic, oh, what I wouldn't do to go back and correct my mistakes of the past! The primary tool for conflict management is to listen to what the other person is saying, regardless of what your stance is. The more you can fight visceral emotion and maintain composure, the more in control and polished you will appear. Write down what the obstacles to coming to an agreement with the other person are, and address them one by one.

If things heat up, respectfully request that the individual stay focused on the subject and not the personalities or emotions involved. It is *never* OK to yell at someone, although I see this happen over and over. The person being yelled at will shut down and stop listening—or worse, scream back. Now you are in a spitting contest as opposed to a business meeting. Try to defuse emotion, and then engage the individual by using supportive phrases: *I can see your point—may I give you mine?* or *I am sorry you feel that way—what would work for you?* or my favorite, *What would make you happy?*

I once dealt with a very difficult manager who had a reputation for bulldozing and intimidating people. His large stature helped him do so. During one discussion, he kept coming at me with negative comment after negative comment, until I felt the room lose all its air and realized it was going to be a toe-to-toe experience. While he ranted and raved, not giving me an inch of room, I waited calmly to speak. My body gestures indicated that I was open but confident, with shoulders squared and feet planted firmly on the ground. I paused in silence, keeping my facial expression neutral to show I was not intimidated, and then asked the question: "Well, you have raised all negative points—so what is your solution?"

He was stumped. He didn't have one. And this made him look foolish, because he had focused on the negative and created a conflict without offering a single real idea. I call this "big hat, no cattle," because he was all talk and no substance. It's an example of how you can easily defuse a situation by simply keeping yourself in check and winning through near silence. It does not always need to be a match of wits to win—just an honest exchange.

Maintain Your Professionalism

We are all familiar with the phrase *Never let them see you sweat*. Use this mantra as a tool when you find yourself in an uncomfortable situation. No matter what the situation, keep your composure—stay in thinking mode. Think of what it's like to watch a great athlete perform, and do your best to exude that same grace under pressure. Pick and choose carefully your professional words, actions, and body language. You can do an autopsy of the conversation later, or even fall apart in the privacy of your own home, but for that moment, that intense period of time, stay in check.

HOW TO ENTERTAIN IN YOUR HOME

For many people, the ultimate test of personal interaction is entertaining business associates at home. This requires a special set of techniques, which may prove to be an essential part of building your professional brand. Bringing your superiors into your home and making them feel comfortable is one of the most powerful career advancement practices you will ever use.

For example, you may find yourself in the position of staging a client or staff party. Holding one of these at your home is terrifying to contemplate but exhilarating to have accomplished. My clients often tell me they would love to entertain, but they find it too overwhelming. My answer is to tackle a home party in the same way you approach a big presentation or project at the office: Build a master plan. My husband used to joke that our house never looked better than before we had a party, because after procrastinating for most of the year, we would work ourselves ragged to clean and repair everything. So here are a few preparatory areas before you dive into execution of the actual event.

Take Care of Repairs

Do a physical walk-through of your home in the months or weeks before your event and decide what needs touch-ups or repairs. It never fails: You will notice *every* imperfection of your home in the days before you host an event. Give yourself enough time to take care of repairs so you can budget and breathe a little more easily.

Be Smart About Invitations

Prepare the guest list, choose invitations, and determine when to send them out. Include such crucial information as *who, what, when,* and *where*. Pay particular attention to the *who,* because protocol can be confusing, especially if multiple levels of executives are attending. You certainly do not want anyone to resent the fact that they were not invited.

Create Flow

Do a mental walk-through: Decide how the party should flow, from the front door and throughout the rest of the space. Where will you greet guests, set up a coat check, and/or place gifts? Go through the motions that a guest would experience, step by step, starting with how visible your street address is from the road and finishing with the guest's reaction to any departure gifts.

Where should the food be available? Map out stations for the food: If you're offering a buffet, also stage nibbles around the house so your guests do not have to fight their way to the trough every time for refreshment.

When considering where to place the bar, remember that it should be built far enough away from the main buffet or any seating areas so that there is no interference between lines of people.

Consider Aesthetics

What about the aesthetics—music, candles, scents, lighting? These are all elements of building an ambience and creating the desired experience. Think carefully about the message that various types of lighting, music, and scents send; these very simple factors can promote the theme for the event and set the stage for the mood of the party. Lively jazz means upbeat and fun, for example, while Sinatra says cool and relaxed.

Set the Table

Do you need to rent china, glassware, and silverware, or do you have the proper inventory? I have gathered an amazing collection over my years of entertaining, but I admit, it is a passion of mine—you might not have the same selection right at home. Do an inventory of your tableware to determine whether it is more cost effective to purchase additional pieces or to rent for that particular event.

Prepare the Menu

Develop an appropriate menu at least one week before the event. If you are working with a caterer, lucky you. If you do need to prepare the food yourself, however, select your menu and then take a step back. Is there the right balance of flavors? If you have three hors d'oeuvres made with cheese, for example, it may be too much. How heavy are the different courses, and do they marry? Once you've ensured that the food reflects balance and harmony, sit down with all the recipes and write the grocery list in groups (vegetables, dairy, meat, etc.) to save you time when you are at the grocery store.

Build In Extra Time

Build a calendar for the week of the event, and divide the workload so you do not feel overwhelmed at the last minute. The point of being a host is to *enjoy* your guests and for your guests to enjoy you. Have you ever attended a party at someone's home and found that the host looked almost miserable because he/she was so tired—or worse, fighting with his/her spouse (there's something about parties that makes you fight with your spouse the week of). If you are frazzled, exhausted, and simply not ready to greet your guests, the party can take on your negative mood. Plan the day by breaking down the timing required for preparation. Time yourself on the preparation of food so you can relax before the actual event. Make as many food items as possible in advance. Finally, leave a two-hour window for yourself so you can relax and get ready.

◆ ◆ ◆

Once you have proved to yourself and your colleagues that you can succeed in business entertaining, you will find that it is extremely rewarding—and a valuable way to build your brand with professionalism.

PRO SCENARIO: INTERACTING WITH COLLEAGUES

Mary is a twenty-five-year-old CPA. After graduating from university about a year ago, she joined a midsize accounting firm. She enjoys the company and is hoping move her way up the ladder.

Traditionally, one of the partners has held the annual holiday party at his home. This year, however, due to a last-minute conflict, he can't play host. Mary, eager to make a good impression, has volunteered to have the event at her house. The partners are appreciative of her offer and gladly accept. With three weeks to plan, Mary feels as though she has plenty of time. She has had friends over many times, for the Super Bowl and backyard picnics. This won't be all that different, right?

Mary did not attend the party last year, but she has heard that the partner always makes a big deal about cooking everything himself and serving as bartender that night. So, Mary figures she had better do the same! She's not an experienced cook, but she starts scouring cook-books and magazines and develops a lavish menu. A couple of days before the party, she gathers up all the recipes and heads to the store. After hours spent running all over town, trying to track down obscure ingredients, she has what she needs.

The morning of the party, she starts to cook. Everything takes quite a bit longer than she anticipated, a couple things don't turn out at all, and at 5:00 p.m. Mary looks up to realize guests will be coming in an hour. She races around to throw together a bar, grabs all the plates and forks she can find, and finishes cooking the food. When the first guests arrive she rushes, disheveled, to the door and lets them in; then she has to go change clothes.

Mary suddenly realizes she has no idea what she is going to wear, and more panic sets in. Twenty minutes later she reappears. More guests have arrived; they've tried to serve themselves drinks, but there are no glasses or ice. Mary notices that the only real noise in the house is coming from her dog, who is running around barking at everyone.

Eventually everyone does get something to eat and drink. They all tell her they had a good time, but the party was certainly not the caliber of those in years past. Most guests leave either feeling sorry for Mary or upset with the company for a "chintzy" party.

What did Mary do wrong?

Where did the company go wrong?

What could Mary have done differently?

For my responses to these questions, visit my website, www.peggynoestevens.com.

SKILL #10
Knowing Your Team

We've worked on skills that strengthen your ability to organize, portray yourself, and present your ideas—and therefore build your confidence and capacity to continuously learn. In this skill, we're going to exercise a different capacity: knowing and having empathy for others as you build a team. Yes, this is a skill that can (and must) be learned. No matter what else you do right, if you can't build relationships or get along with people, your personal brand is going to fail.

I did not write this book as a management guru or an academic, but as a coach. Research makes it clear that communication, collaboration, and all manner of social interaction are key to business performance. Access to the Internet and news media, in addition to individual training and education, means we have mobile, flexible, social people in our workplaces who want to be informed and connected. We need to pay attention.

GENERAL GUIDELINES

As you build a team, remember the three general guidelines listed below.

They will prove beneficial in developing deeper relationships and avoiding counterproductive negativity in the workplace.

Get to Know Your Colleagues

Your team members are not members of your family or your close-knit circle, but still they are human beings with whom you will need to spend a lot of time. For the most part they share common vulnerabilities, fears, and hopes. Life is pretty simple, someone once said, until you throw people into it. Our personalities and skill sets are unique, and it takes patience and sincere outreach to build a strong foundation. Once you make the effort to build it, your colleagues can become your biggest champions in the workplace.

Everybody Has a Right to Be Heard

Your team members deserve to be listened to, to be reassured, and to have a sense of purpose at work—these are human needs. It is our nature to have low energy and even become depressed if we are placed in the role of an outcast who does not have a secure place within the tribe. This need to belong is part of who we are as humans. It is part of how we evolved and how we are nurtured. Remember the punishments of elementary school? *Go to the principal's office. Go sit in the corner.* When you consistently signal to a team member or colleague that his/her concerns don't matter to you, that the person is less significant or not valued as a tribe member, you will see the inevitable result. It starts with the averted gaze and slumped shoulders, like those of the classmate no one likes, and continues with a lack of energy, curiosity, and engagement. A team member who doesn't participate and produce is not useful to you or your professional goals.

Deal Effectively with Influencers

Being the target of what I like to call "influencers" is a huge hurdle to overcome when forming an effective team. Influencers are the bold folks who spread gossip and rumors, even when they are not true, with authority and casualness. Being the victim of an influencer is tricky because these people create a hole—one that you did not necessarily dig for yourself, one that is unbeknownst to you but that does damage nonetheless.

When considering influencers, it is important to differentiate between "flyers" and "buyers." *Flyers* are the influencers in the locker room who just "fly by" people with information, good or bad, that influences perceptions of others. They are dangerous because they speak with ease and then move on without a care in the world, never taking into account the damage they can do. *Buyers* are at the opposite end of the scope—the listeners and the receivers of the flyers' information. They are like sponges, soaking in the information, forming opinions without facts or evidence to back them up. The challenge is to teach buyers to give the benefit of the doubt, to reject rumors that don't hold up, and to defend the honor of someone who is the object of gossip.

SPECIFIC TECHNIQUES

Now that you understand the general guidelines for getting to know the people on your team, here are some specific techniques for putting yourself in their shoes. These methods will help you as you consider how to manage your team.

Avoid the Blame Game

Always take the emotion out of situations that place blame. Trying to figure out *Whose fault is it?* is one of the most dangerous games you can play. Blame is perhaps the number one destroyer in business. Please don't get me wrong: Accountability is important. But you must know the difference between managing an issue in order to reach the business goal or project and wasting valuable time by backtracking to see who is to blame. It is not *who* is right but rather *what* is right. When dealing with the *who,* be a marriage counselor and listen intently to both sides. Then decide the right thing to do—*what* will benefit everyone and not just one person. I had a great boss who, no matter how difficult his employees were, always found the good in them (even when I could not). I admired that.

Provide a Purpose

Let employees understand the purpose of their tasks. If I asked you today, could you answer these questions: What is the core purpose of your work? What is your *raison d'être* (reason for being)? When I do strategic sessions for clients, I always ask these questions. It never ceases to amaze me that people have to stop and think hard before answering. When you're dedicated to the work you do, the answers should roll off your tongue! I was intrigued recently by an HR employee of a major client of mine. When asked that question, she answered it in a New York minute, voluntarily complimenting senior managers on their enthusiasm and vision. She was in tune with the big picture, as if she were single-handedly carrying out the order! I think you would understand why, if you ever visited the company's corporate offices and saw the incredibly well-done, inspirational environment. It screams, *Mission! Vision! Purpose!* As a twenty-plus-year veteran of the corporate arena, I assure you that I know "bull malarkey" when I see it. This woman was real, and I was impressed by the company leadership.

Offer Ownership

Why should anyone be motivated when they get nothing from the results? When you manage in a vacuum, not sharing information or your vision, your people are working in the dark—there is no visibility or understanding of the *why* behind the daily tasks and responsibilities. On the other hand, when you allow your employees to be part of the vision and share the big-picture goals, they buy into the plan and accept a sense of ownership. They act as if they are directly responsible for the success of the company (which they are), and this will always produce better results.

Teach Abundance

I always work at a higher level when I know my hard work will indeed pay off. Giving employees the gift of abundance—the wide-open field of opportunity, incentives, recognition, awards—is key to creating the sense of self-satisfaction that will motivate them. When there are no golden rings, there is nothing to grab but complacency. When there is something in it for everyone, your team will aspire to reach new heights and achieve the goals you set for them.

Be Diplomatic

When your credibility and professionalism are on the line, saying "You really pissed me off!" won't get you far. It is difficult but essential that you find the most diplomatic words and delivery possible; this will help you avoid eruptions (both your own and the team's). Get to the point of what you are trying to communicate, but also consider how you will be perceived by your team. I train people to use the mantra *Think, speak, think.* That is, *think* about how to deliver the message, then *speak* the message, and then *think* about the reaction you receive from the individual—how the message was perceived and whether it will be retained. A careful choice of words can make all the difference in the world. Here are a few examples:

> Don't say, *You pissed me off.* Instead say, *I think this was a bit upsetting.*
>
> Don't say, *You lied about that.* Instead say, *Did I misinterpret your message?*
>
> Don't say, *You screwed up.* Instead say, *Let's take a minute to figure this out.*

Don't Jump to Conclusions

Never make decisions using a crystal ball to try to predict the outcome based on third-party information. Third-party information, although sometimes reliable, can also be inflated to lead you to think that you have been wronged. Carefully evaluate the information, but more important, the source from which it came.

Watch Your Tone

Always be aware of the voice and tone you use, as the right delivery can promote bonding with your team members. We covered voice in Skill #1 and Skill #7, but to reiterate: For effective delivery, your words need to match the cadence, tone, and voice you use.

Never Tolerate a Bully

Schools today have truly embraced antibullying programs, because bullying is severely damaging to children. One oversight in the adult world is not recognizing the need for an antibullying program in the workplace. Bullies (and you know who they are) intimidate, mock, steamroll, and destroy people—typically because they have a deep psychological disconnect that prevents them from being able to deal with others. They are always on the defensive, in ego-protection mode, and will take someone out at a moment's notice if they perceive a threat.

When you are constantly fearful of someone, have lost sleep over the way you have been treated repeatedly by an individual, or feel harassed and excluded because of just one person—you need to take action. One thing I learned as a female businessperson is to recognize a bully. You will always work with high-energy, demanding people, and you must learn how to handle difficult people in certain situations. The difference between a demanding person and a bully is that a bully will try to destroy your reputation, sabotage your work, or exploit his/her authority over you (no matter how minor) in order to see you crawl off to a corner and lick your wounds. People who are affected by bullying tend to display the persona of a battered spouse. As a coach, I sometimes find myself in a position of addressing the low self-esteem and damage caused by a bully and the effect they have on the employee.

My experience has taught me a few things in this regard. First, always strive for diplomacy. Try your best to find out what the bully's hot buttons are and avoid them; instead find common ground where you can make the bully comfortable with you. Focusing on similar interests instead of disconnects and conflict sometimes gains a bully's trust. Second, if you are exhausted by diplomacy and this tool is not working no matter how hard you have tried, then punch the bully in the mouth—figuratively, of course, with your words. Read about any children's antibullying program, and you'll learn that most bullies are really frightened or deeply wounded themselves. When you stand up to a bully and let the person know what you think of his/her behavior and how it needs to change, oddly enough, sometimes he or she will back down.

As a last resort, if absolutely nothing is working for you and the bully is affecting your thinking process or emotional well-being, report the person to a higher authority. Hopefully, your company has a process and policies in place to prevent bullying. Sometimes bullies crumble only when a bigger hammer comes down on them. Be prepared to give documented examples of bullying, and know that doing so will demonstrate that the person has been bullying you. Remember that you have to live with yourself—you are the only one who can decide whether you approve of yourself. I would rather stand my ground and hold on to my self-respect than let a bully defeat me. It helps me sleep at night.

✦ ✦ ✦

Your personal brand depends on people, and the people on your team are your core constituency for promoting that brand. As your career develops and you find yourself in the role of leader, you will need to expand your horizons to include a better understanding of and improved communication with people. The guidelines and techniques for connecting with your team members will serve you well in maintaining and evolving your brand.

 ## PRO SCENARIO: KNOWING YOUR TEAM

Brenda is the manager of a large team at a construction firm. She has been with the company for seven years, and despite a few challenges, she has done a pretty good job. Brenda takes pride in the fact that she sticks to the guidelines yet remains friendly with her colleagues.

Feeling ready to move up, Brenda applies for a director position at the firm, but she does not get the job. Instead, the firm hires David, a young, experienced manager from another firm. Brenda is livid.

Over the next couple of weeks, David evaluates Brenda's department. He determines that although Brenda is very capable in many ways, she isn't working toward any improvements. He sees some opportunities for development and feels that changes are desperately needed to ensure the company's overall growth.

Upset by all the changes David is making, Brenda turns to her co-workers, the people whom she sees as her friends. She doesn't understand how someone so new can make so many changes so quickly. She feels as though it isn't his place to deliver news of the changes to her team, as surely they would rather hear it from her. Brenda cannot say enough bad things about David to anyone who will listen. Whenever they meet, she gets defensive with him, often raising her voice.

David doesn't understand why everyone at this new company

seems to welcome him except for Brenda. He truly feels that Brenda's strong commitment to the company and the relationships she has with her team are assets, but he knows she speaks poorly of him with their colleagues. He decides to talk with her, but she is not interested. In fact, Brenda tells David that she has found work with a competitor and will be leaving the company because she is unhappy.

What happened?

What could Brenda have done differently?

What lessons can you apply?

For my responses to these questions, visit my website, www.peggynoestevens.com.

SKILL #11

COMMUNICATING WITH TRANSPARENCY

Being a good leader means understanding that folks are self-interested but that you can't let your own self-interest be the only thing that guides you. In the corporate world, even alligators smile. If you have ever felt the sting of an unexpected "sniper" at work, or been floored by an individual who threw you under the proverbial bus, you have experienced the antithesis of transparency.

You have probably heard the expression *He's hard to read* and wondered why people don't just say what they mean. When you cloak your views and positions in vague or misleading language, you run the risk of being misunderstood. If you tell people what they want to hear instead of what they need to hear, you might lose your co-workers' trust. Although you may not be aware of it, by maintaining a pose that is less than genuine, you let people know that you are hiding your intentions; this makes them uncomfortable around you, because they don't know what your goals are. And this has a negative impact on your personal brand.

Transparency is an essential ingredient in developing leadership skills and relationships. Transparency is about appearing sincere and saying what you mean, with no hidden agenda, so that others accept you at face value. This does not mean you should feel free to deliver overly critical or hurtful messages. It means you must use clear, neutral, unemotional language without confusion and subterfuge. You must remain open and forthcoming, even when the not-so-great message needs to be delivered. Transparent people know how to communicate swiftly and diplomatically. This is the essence of leadership.

DEVELOPING PROPER WORKPLACE INTERACTIONS

Transparency in workplace interactions saves valuable time, because it allows you to understand any communication the first time. Have you ever walked away from a conversation and then thought to yourself, *I wonder what he/she meant by that?* As you review the following situations, compare the characteristic "hiding" message with the transparent or "open" message.

> **Situation 1:** The team leader changes a meeting. He/she says . . .
>
> **Hiding message:** We need to reschedule the meeting.
>
> **Transparent message:** I'm running behind schedule, and I apologize for the inconvenience.

> **Situation 2:** You ask the boss about your work performance. He/she says . . .
>
> **Hiding message:** You are doing fine.

Transparent message: I feel that your work is on par but could be better.

Situation 3: You've tried a daring outfit, and you run into your manager in the hallway. He/she says . . .

Hiding message: What an interesting outfit!

Transparent message: I don't think your clothes are appropriate for the workplace.

Situation 4: You stop by the boss's office a few times to check on a key matter. You say . . .

Hiding message: You seem really busy.

Transparent message: You are not paying attention to me. Is something wrong?

Do you see the difference between transparent and hidden communication? Consider the likely implications of sending the wrong message when you are not being transparent. It is critical that you develop the skill of using transparent communication when connecting with members of your team.

TRANSPARENT COMMUNICATION TECHNIQUES

To develop your personal brand as a leader, you must understand the value of being clear and presenting an authentic message. The following are some techniques for taking a transparent approach to various tasks and responsibilities.

Time Management

Credible managers let everyone know where they stand regarding this vital resource; they know who has enough time to take on more duties and who is already swamped. If someone on your team—or even you or your boss—is drowning in work and the hamster wheel just keeps on spinning, you must speak up. Redistribute the work, or acknowledge that you may need another game plan. People often are afraid to speak up about their workload because they feel that their position could be in jeopardy if they appear to be complaining. But if you take the right approach, the opposite can be true: You will look like a proactive and strategic thinker by being transparent to your boss about the tasks you have completed, what remains to be done in the long term, and finally what possible solutions you suggest. Rather than suffer in silence, speak up about managing time and resist too much work.

Work Roles

Communicate duties and responsibilities clearly with your colleagues. Your team members need to know their roles so they can concentrate on them. Confusion in this area is one of the most common complaints I hear from employees, because many times people's roles evolve and things are added to their plate over time—and before you know it, the job has morphed into a totally different role. When duplication of effort is evident, or when nothing is being done because "I thought she was in charge of that," it is time to sit down and review roles and responsibilities.

Personal Presence

Be in touch with your posture, your vocal quality, and your eye contact. Words must meet actions and vice versa. Use your body language effectively so your people can read you clearly, and try to read their body language. For example, if someone says she accepts the situation, but her face is turning red and she's gritting her teeth as she speaks, her behavior does not match her speech; you can be sure that her spoken message is not transparent. When people's words do not match their actions, pause and question the response. It can even help to ask an open-ended question, such as *Do you still have some questions that I may answer for you?*

Preparation

Credible leaders take as long to prepare as necessary and make it clear what preparation is required to be successful. Don't just jump into an assigned project; as a leader, you need to obtain or develop a road map and deadlines. Then answer each question on what I call the "W" list:

- *Who* needs to work with me on the project? Whom should I enlist in the process?
- *What* needs to be done in terms of goals, output, and methodology?
- *When* does the project need to be complete? What checkpoints along the way can help determine whether we are on target?
- *Where* are we taking the project after completion? What is the presentation and communication schedule?

The questions are clear and purposeful; they help you think ahead about the project and prevent you from just looking in the rearview mirror. Transparent communication provides good direction.

✦ ✦ ✦

Effective and authentic communication is essential as your career develops and you acquire more responsibility. Communication skills are part of the foundation on which you will build your brand within your organization. The best leaders are transparent in their communication and do not leave the employee guessing what he/she may need or want.

 ## PRO SCENARIO: COMMUNICATING WITH TRANSPARENCY

Rebecca is an up-and-coming designer. She started her design studio by herself, but she became popular quickly and hired Emily as her assistant.

Emily is not a designer herself; she has a marketing background. She has decided that she is interested in the fashion industry and has committed to starting at the bottom in order to work her way up. Rebecca is not quite sure how to use Emily, but knows that Emily can help.

Emily dives right in by requesting that the two of them sit down and outline expectations. Before long, Emily is organizing fabric, taking care of Rebecca's schedule, answering the phones, and making appointments to meet with vendors and retailers. Emily does everything she is asked and then some. She and Rebecca often meet to discuss ideas, and she feels free to share her own, some of which help the business become successful.

Over a few years, the company grows until eventually it is a multi-million-dollar business. Rebecca, realizing that she could not have obtained this level of success without Emily, promotes her to vice president of marketing. Emily, now needing help herself, hires Jonathan to assist her.

Jonathan has a background in the fashion industry and feels he will be a major asset to the company. As it turns out, however, he becomes a problem for the company. He offers no input at meetings, he rarely gets his work done on time, and he complains about his salary to his friends. When Emily asks Jonathan if he is happy with his work, though, Jonathan tells her that he is.

Jonathan is perfectly capable of doing his job, but he certainly has not operated at a level that contributes to the success of the company. He works for Emily for about a year and then quits.

What did Jonathan do wrong?

Could Emily or Rebecca have done something differently to change the outcome?

What could Jonathan have done differently?

What lessons can you apply?

For my responses to these questions, visit my website, www.peggynoestevens.com.

SKILL #12
MANAGING WITH HOSPITALITY

In addition to interacting with the people on your team or subordinates within your organization, you will also have to learn how to deal successfully with those who outrank you. The most successful way to burnish your brand in these types of interactions is to manage with hospitality.

I began my career in the field of hospitality working for the Hyatt Hotels Corporation. I remember my first job out of college as a sort of hospitality boot camp; I worked fifty to sixty hours a week, all hours of the day and night. It was about fast-paced thinking and grace under pressure—traits I learned and carried over to the rest of my career. We saw it as a badge of honor when a client wrote to the general manager of the hotel about his or her experience. This kind of positive feedback from guests mattered at evaluation time. I was pleased to know that guests had appreciated my work, and I came to learn that the hospitality profession is always defined by guests, service, and satisfaction.

After I left Hyatt, I found that these values informed my success in meeting my goals: I always treated executives and managers as valued clients. I worked with a sense of urgency, wore a positive disposition, arrived early (or on time), and made listening to others a priority—all elements of hospitality.

Later on in my career, as corporate colleagues would complain that delivering service for the boss or senior executives amounted to brownnosing, I viewed my work through a different prism. I delivered service that exceeded expectations: I wanted that letter written on my behalf.

In speech after speech and session after session as an executive coach, I've learned that hospitality is a metaphor that sticks for service and performance. Even today, my staff knows our creed: *If we do what you expected, then we have failed.* In other words, the goal is to surprise people with the results because you did more than they expected.

TECHNIQUES FOR MANAGING WITH HOSPITALITY

The following techniques will help you manage with service and professionalism in mind.

Deliver Surprising Service

Always know the expectations and outline your plan to achieve them. Then take a step back and ask, "What more can I deliver that is of value, above and beyond the expected? What extra effort could result in a positive response?"

Use Peripheral Vision

Always be aware of the customer, who in this case is your boss. I have expressed the importance of getting the "human read" by understanding nonverbal gestures, but exercising your peripheral vision on your surroundings is perhaps even more important. The human read may mean focusing on one individual as you speak with him or her, but using peripheral vision means still being aware of what is going on in the room around you and, in particular, people's reactions to what you are saying—silence, laughter, and so forth. What is the energy of the room and its people? Who is talking with whom at a meeting? Which people are friends, and who does not get along? Who is having a bad day in the office? What is the reaction of folks when you walk into a room? The more you are self-aware and pick up signals, messages, and facial expressions, the better. Think of the hospitality industry, where employees must be attentive to the needs and gestures of their customers.

Be Urgent

Always rely on a sense of urgency when accomplishing a task. You want to express a sense of purpose and an understanding of the task's significance. Whatever deadline is given to you, exceed the expectations by marking a date earlier than what was assigned. It shows pride in getting a job completed efficiently.

Anticipate Needs

Always anticipate the needs of your boss, and stay ahead of them. Truly understanding your manager's workload can reveal what you can do to assist him/her and give you a heads-up on suggested projects that interest you. If your manager calls you for a meeting and you know the agenda topics ahead of time, do some background or research to better prepare yourself; this will convey your interest and show that you are aggressive about understanding the landscape.

Organize Your Calendar

Always organize your calendar to work 30-60-90 days out. Many hospitality communities work on a 30-60-90-day calendar to forecast clients, events, VIP visits, etc., so they are prepared and focused the day of the customer's visit. All projects require project management, or timelines. Again, understand the delivery date and then go back into the project, setting milestones and review dates so that you can stay on task. You will better understand what is coming up, how much you need to manage your workload, and how to block out time to actually work on the task at hand.

◆ ◆ ◆

By practicing management with hospitality, you will be able to develop a positive relationship with your bosses. Even if you are confident in that relationship, however, you will still need to master certain skills for what may be the most difficult interaction with superiors: the performance review, covered in Skill #13.

PRO SCENARIO: MANAGING WITH HOSPITALITY

Scott works as a front desk manager for a popular hotel chain. He's an intelligent, ambitious person, and he has dedicated many years to working in the hotel industry. He always gets the job done, going above and beyond to make the guests happy. He loves where he works. In fact, Scott would really like to be the general manager of this particular property.

Scott manages a team of six people including Jessica, the hotel's newly promoted reservationist. Jessica really deserves her new job. After working in an entry-level position at the hotel for nearly five years, she is ready for this new challenge. She's a hard worker and, just like Scott, has high aspirations for herself with the company. This new position will require training in an area where she has no previous experience.

This is where Scott comes in. As Jessica's manager, he is responsible for training her—but instead of doing so, he takes on the work himself. Now, whenever Jessica attempts to question Scott, they end up in an argument and Scott storms off, feeling frustrated at Jessica's lack of understanding.

Thus begins the chatter in the break room. Apparently, other employees feel the same way about him. They say that he is difficult to approach and they never know what he expects of them until a mistake has been made.

The hotel continues to operate successfully despite these conditions. Jessica and her co-workers move forward, doing the best they can while also trying to avoid Scott, which periodically leads to preventable mistakes. Not only does Jessica essentially train herself, she offers support to the rest of the team—never complaining, but rather trying to promote a positive work environment. Scott doesn't know this, but Jessica would eventually like to move up into the position of front desk manager.

Scott's team is frustrated, and so is Scott.

One day, the position of general manager opens up. Scott is highly qualified for this role. He feels that this is the break he needs and deserves—and yet Scott does not get the job.

Why didn't Scott get the promotion to general manager?

What could Scott have done differently? What lessons can you apply?

For my responses to these questions, visit my website, www.peggynoestevens.com.

SKILL #13
SURVIVING A PERFORMANCE REVIEW

Death, taxes, and performance reviews—these are life's unavoidable moments of accountability. You will either be giving or receiving performance reviews (or both) for your entire working life. Performance reviews are the ultimate test of your brand as it is perceived by other people. The more you understand how to own and drive the process, from either side of the desk, the better the results will be for you.

When you are being reviewed, remember that only you can be in charge of your career. It is your responsibility to gather and present information in your favor, to "make your case." Can you think of anyone else you can count on to do that essential work? About three weeks before a review is scheduled, begin collecting and analyzing information on your performance metrics so that you are prepared to present your case during the review.

As a manager, urge your direct reports to take this approach as well. Anyone who researches his/her performance in this way will better understand his/her progress and accomplishments against various goals and objectives and will be able to envision the areas where improvement is necessary. Your team members will begin to own the results and their implications.

In most cases, employees who have been passed over for a promotion or even let go don't understand why. Corporate politics, economics, mergers and acquisitions—all these play their part. I am suggesting, however, that you stop guessing how you are doing and take action instead.

TECHNIQUES FOR SURVIVING A PERFORMANCE REVIEW

Communication and clarity are crucial when using the following techniques to deal with a performance review. Don't allow evaluations to creep up on you. Leave time to prepare and build your backdrop for the accomplishments you have achieved. Also leave time for yourself to correct any areas that have not been accomplished. The timing of your reviews could be quarterly, semiannual, or annual. No matter the frequency, allow for prep time before each.

Know the Metrics

Always understand how you are being measured: What goals, objectives, and tasks have been outlined for you? Is there a timeline for completion of those aspects? Your company may have an annual evaluation form with competencies and language that are specific to the company. Make sure you know what the form says and what this means for you. All too often I have heard from employees who felt they did a fabulous job, only to find out during an evaluation that they missed the mark and failed to deliver what their boss really wanted from them. There is no greater waste of time than a great job that did not need to be done.

Focus on the Tangibles

Always elaborate on how you achieved the goals, through examples, financials, statistics, and outcomes. Concrete, tangible examples are truly effective during a performance review. Hard facts, specific results, and descriptions help paint the picture of what you achieved. Should you include *all* available tangibles in your communication? Maybe not, but I would have examples close at hand in case you are questioned on the results that you achieved.

Another area to think about is *how* the results were achieved. Did you work solo? Lead a team and build new relationships? Or steamroll everyone into thinking your way? Decide on the description that best paints the picture for you, and back it up with cold, hard facts.

Seek Training

Always ask what needs to happen for you to become a better-trained employee. What are the competencies required for your job—or better yet for the job you aspire to have one day? By taking the initiative on training, you show you are willing to grow. It is sometimes difficult to know what you do not know, so be sure to ask about what you might be missing. Even the most useful training can be overwhelming or boring and cumbersome, but if it is important to your company, then it is important to you as well. Talk to others in your company (perhaps a mentor or someone who did your job before you) and find out what they would have done differently when it came to training. Take suggestions and feedback, and then map your training plan. Be realistic, and try not to overdo it. Don't spend more time in training classes than you spend working at your job!

Build a Road Map

Always build a road map, in cooperation with your boss, so you can track your career path and aspire to the next job. Still, it is crucial not to get too far ahead of yourself with career aspirations; maybe you have yet to prove that you are capable of your current job. Focus on this achievement first, and then when you have demonstrated competence and measured results, be prepared to continue along the career path you've mapped out.

Ask your HR department or your boss about the natural progression for your career, considering the role that you are in. You may also identify other departments of interest and roles that you could see yourself morphing into. My all-time favorite career advancements have been when I saw a gap in the company structure and was given the creative license to create a new job based on company needs. Not only did this appeal to my entrepreneurial spirit and give me incredible ownership, but also it showcased my initiative and awareness.

Check In

In addition to the annual review, it is important that you have more frequent check-ins with your reviewer. The performance review should not be the only occasion for getting thorough feedback on your job performance. Instead, check in quarterly to measure your performance against your plan and to ensure that you are on track. Setting and reaching mileposts will allow you to remain flexible as you navigate through the year and help you avoid surprises when the annual review is performed.

It will certainly happen sometimes that things do not go your way during a check-in, but be fearless about receiving this feedback, because it may be what sets you apart in the long run. After all, you embraced the self-knowledge and were professionally mature enough to try harder and improve upon your faults. More than likely, your manager will be impressed with your personal candor and sincere desire to do better in all areas; he or she may even disagree, praising you where you thought you'd done poorly. What a bonus!

 ## PRESENCE PRACTICE

If you were to build a short list of your accomplishments and a short list of areas that need improvement, would they be evenly matched? Striving for excellence usually means not only celebrating your strengths, but also being introspective about weaker areas and how you might improve them.

No one is a perfect employee; we all have weaknesses and we all have strengths. Take the good medicine with the bad, and never let the bad define who you are. Change it, accept it, or discard the information, but never let it define you or your brand.

 ## PRO SCENARIO: SURVIVING A PERFORMANCE REVIEW

Julie has worked at a large automotive plant for fifteen years when her boss retires and is replaced by Steve. Steve has decided that, in an effort to get to know his employees and make sure that their department is operating efficiently, he will implement performance reviews. Julie is offended about being called in for a review. She sees it as being asked to defend her job, which she doesn't feel she should have to do; after all, she has given the company fifteen years of service!

"Do they think I'm doing something wrong?" Julie complains to her co-workers.

On the morning of the review, Julie is ready to go to battle. Steve welcomes her into his office with a warm smile, asking first about her family, her time with the company, her outside interests. He is generally interested in getting to know her.

Julie isn't buying it, especially when Steve goes on to say he doesn't feel that Julie has been challenging herself in her role with the company. He also mentions that he feels she gossips at work, which promotes a negative attitude around her. In conclusion, Steve tells Julie that she is an asset to the company and he looks forward to working with her.

Julie, steaming mad over the imperfect review, barely hears the positive parts and declines to respond at all. Instead, she walks out and works unhappily for the next few weeks—until she decides to quit because she has a new boss who is just terrible.

What did Julie do wrong?

What could Julie have done differently?

What lessons can you apply?

For my responses to these questions, visit my website, www.peggynoestevens.com.

PART IV
SUMMARY

There is no more important concept in this book than the one on which part IV is based: It is all about the people . . . it is all about the people . . . it is all about the people. (Am I making myself clear?) Putting the right people behind you, in front of you, and alongside you will carry you to success.

My very best friend's mother, who was like a second mother to me, used to tell me that if I could name five close friends on one hand, I would have the world by a string. She may have been referring to personal friendships, but I am happy to report that this holds true in the workplace, too. When people like you, they will promote you without you ever being aware of it. They become your champions. Having these supporters is helpful during a talent review or evaluation, because your boss will know how others feel about your contributions.

On the flip side, can you list on one hand the number of people with whom you have destroyed a relationship? I sure hope it's not over the limit of five, and if it is, you need to ask why. What could you be doing to improve that relationship instead? Win back the people you have lost, and keep building your person-to-person repertoire as you build your career.

Aspire to be a transparent communicator and to manage your work with ownership and hospitality, and you will build champions for your brand.

CONCLUSION:
PUTTING IT ALL TOGETHER

OVERVIEW

Now that you have learned how to create your own brand, you must learn how to synchronize your personal brand with your organization's brand. The most important criterion to remember as you look at your brand and the company brand is to embrace characteristics of the culture of the company, but while doing so, never eclipse your own brand by becoming a walking billboard for the company. Why? Because you will lose your authenticity and be branded as a poser. Companies hire people for their unique assets and capabilities. Yes, they look at fit as well—whether you will fit with the culture of the company—but I assure you that you were hired because you have something to offer that is uniquely yours. And this you want to keep!

"A brand is a living entity," observed Michael Eisner, former CEO of Disney, "and it is enriched or undermined cumulatively over time, the product of a thousand small gestures." The brand you project every day, consciously or unconsciously, affects the brand of the organization where you work. Give it some thought.

What is the essence of your organization's brand? What words would you use to define it? Consider these global firms and some words that define their brand essence:

- Nike: Authentic athletic performance
- Disney: Fun, family entertainment that appeals to the child in each of us
- Starbucks: Rewarding, everyday moments
- Jeep: Rugged, timeless, American

These famous brands tell a story that people want to talk about and participate in. Like any great story, a brand story is true and trusted. It is subtle, and it makes a promise. When we experience a great brand, we contribute our own stories.

Consider the Disney brand and the stories that many Americans share and hold in our minds about taking young kids on their first trip to Disneyland. When we enter the park, we're going to find that the myriad details surrounding us confirm the brand experience we expect. The rides and attractions will be working. The Disney actors will be in costume. The gift stores will be open. The service will be excellent. We know, expect, and trust that Disney will orchestrate the vast, sweeping myriad of features that make up the Disneyland experience. We will experience that story and later have our own story to tell. These details are in place because Disney employees are aware of their brand's essence, and they know how they contribute to it through their own personal brand.

Whatever your position or your business, you can expand your brand sense as you promote the company's brand. Advertising, social media, and graphic design are part of a brand identity, but only you can provide the human element to your organization's brand. Think of yourself as a brand ambassador.

How can you strengthen your own brand by synchronizing with your organization's brand?

SKILL #14

SYNCHRONIZING YOUR PERSONAL BRAND WITH YOUR ORGANIZATION'S BRAND

Creating an understanding of the company brand and the culture and environment in which you work corresponds with the way you develop your personal brand within the company. If you do not understand the business or industry in which you work, the environment and landscape of the people, it will be difficult to understand where you fit.

WHAT YOU NEED TO DO (INTERNALLY)

You may need to become your own researcher, to a certain degree, to fully contribute to the company and serve as its ambassador. Here are some tips on how to collect the data you need for your internal knowledge base.

Commit to Continuous Learning

Understand the culture of your company. Do you know and understand the history of the company, its icons within the industry, and the evolution of building its brand? The best way to anchor your knowledge in the present is by understanding the past. Treat it like a research project, and keep a file of clips, historical notes, and significant milestones.

Another great way to understand who's who is to look at the organizational chart. I know this sounds obvious, but many of my clients do not know the company hierarchy or the other departments that make the big company engine run. Not understanding how all the parts and pieces come together makes it difficult to navigate your career and to network within your company. During any conference I ever coordinated as an event planner, I would show photographs of the executive committee to the hotel staff; this way, they would recognize a VIP and treat him/her with due respect—and it proved very helpful to the staff. If I showed you pictures of your company's executive team, would you know who they were?

Read Voraciously

Never stop reading about the industry you are in. Knowledge about your industry not only will help you truly understand the business, but it could also spark your creativity by helping you identify what the industry is in need of—what gaps you might help fill.

Study the Market

There may be a reason that the company did not give out raises this year, so instead of complaining, ask yourself whether you understand the landscape of the economy and market environment.

Become a Customer

Put yourself in the customer's shoes, and imagine yourself as a customer who uses your company's products or services. Essentially, this means you should try to "walk the talk." Familiarizing yourself with the products you handle will truly help you understand the consumer's side of things. Have you met a consumer who has experienced your product recently? What did this person say, and what about that commentary offers insights into the brand? If you do have the luxury of sampling or using your company's brand(s), then you have a distinct advantage.

Now begin thinking of what the brand needs are, and then apply those needs to your job responsibility. Identify and share key words that define your organization's brand(s): your brand essence. This is similar to identifying your personal brand; if someone were asked to describe you, what would immediately come to mind? Understanding the descriptors given helps you to identify your brand essence.

WHAT YOU NEED TO DO (EXTERNALLY)

You have a great deal to learn about your brand and your organization's brand from external sources as well. To synchronize the two brands, casually collect information from friends, customers, and anyone else who is connected with your organization to build your knowledge.

Get Feedback

Talk to peers and friends about the company brand. When working with a client, I always like to talk to employees who have been with the company for at least five years, to gain an understanding of the perceptions and opinions of people who usually have a good sense of the company culture. Understanding the culture helps you understand how your personal brand fits into an organization. I also listen intently for what the client likes and admires about the company—and for negative clips or frustrations—to guide me. Yes, even negative clips need to be heard. You do not need to always agree, but it's important to just listen and then form your own opinions.

Study Perspective

Study how consumers, peers, and senior managers experience your product, service, or facility. Every six months, work out in detail the experience of your brand—I am talking about your personal brand and the company product you represent—from a customer's perspective. Ask team members to give their opinion of the brand and the response they receive from consumers. Incorporate the customer's experience you attempted to understand as part of the internal requirements.

Most important, when trying to understand perspectives, make sure your customer interactions are informative and useful. How do you do this?

Cultivate relationship moments

This can be as casual as running into a friend at a party and asking his or her opinion of the product. You are starting a dialogue about the person's relationship to the product. When I founded an association called Bourbon Women, it was the first women's consumer organization in the beverage industry. Although I felt that I knew the target market of females, instead of just making an educated guess I began conversations with women I knew who loved bourbon. These conversations eventually formalized into focus groups, then a strategy session with a handpicked board of directors, and then, voilà! Bourbon Women was born. Although my instincts were on target, I learned because I listened and gave these new members what they asked for instead of what we thought they would like. There is a difference, you know?

Learn names

Get to know your customers. Share news about yourself—internally with your boss or HR department—but don't overdo it, or it will look like shameless self-promotion. Instead, give small, frequent feedings—just enough to keep you on their radar. Your co-workers and customers will be impressed with how you take the initiative. Go beyond names by mapping out a plan to meet and network with all departments in a company. This will give you insight into your fellow employees' or the customer's perspective and offer a clearer vision of your role.

Organize the process

Manage the work processes to incorporate employee contacts as well as customer interactions and experiences. Set a twelve-month calendar that rotates appointments with your contacts—one department each month. Just one lunch a month with someone new can make a difference. Map out your evaluations, and give yourself time to prepare for quarterly or annual reviews. Perhaps you don't have the luxury of meeting with your boss or an important client every day or even weekly; if a significant amount of time goes by and you have not seen him/her, then make a concerted effort to place yourself on the person's calendar so you can catch up on various projects.

Empower team members

Your team should become a group of "emotional engines." Be aware of how others feel and of the impact that the day-to-day environment has on the team. Touch base with the entire team, or plan an activity that is enjoyable and not work related, so team members can get to know each other on a personal basis. Give credit where credit is due, and celebrate team successes. Hold meetings to distribute work with the expectations that each individual is empowered to perform and deliver results; showing your confidence in your team will help them to "own" their work. When a boss trusts an employee to perform his/her job and gets out of the way rather than being too hands-on, the benefits are immeasurable.

Refine your brand

Continuously refine your own brand. Be a maniac for excellence. As Walmart founder Sam Walton once said, "Excellence can be irritating," because it is constant and fluid. It is not about being perfect; it's about making positive changes based on good feedback. Improving your brand is like investing in a 401(k): The payoff will come in the long term.

◆ ◆ ◆

Synchronicity between your personal brand and your organization's brand is the ultimate goal of the professional presence. After you have completed the process described in this book, your brand will be so strong that it will add to your organization's brand. This creates a powerful brand-building feedback loop that will in time ensure your career success.

 ## PRO SCENARIO: SYNCHRONIZING YOUR PERSONAL BRAND WITH YOUR ORGANIZATION'S BRAND

Stacey is the human resources manager for a healthy sports drink company. She is a great role model at work. She encourages her employees to keep an active lifestyle and support the brand they sell. If asked, Stacey would say that she loves the product and she loves what she does—but you would never know it, because you never see the drink in her hand when she's away from the office. In fact, Stacey's friends know her less as a professional and instead as a great friend and mother and an avid runner.

One day, while Stacey is sitting in the stands at her son's baseball game, another parent whom she often sees at games mentions that he wishes they carried his favorite energy drink. It happens to be the one that Stacey's company sells. Embarrassed, Stacey admits that she works for the company he has mentioned but doesn't know why the park doesn't carry its product.

What is Stacey doing wrong?

What should Stacey do differently?

What lessons can you apply?

For my responses to these questions, visit my website, www.peggynoestevens.com.

CONCLUSION

SUMMARY

It is my greatest hope that learning about the skills outlined in this book will lead you to build an effective personal brand. Embrace the model of professional presence in your dealings with people in order to fully move in the direction of building relationships with your boss, managers, peers, and staff. Your presence and brand will always be your calling card. How do you wish people to remember you?

What a wonderful business world we would have if everyone moved in the direction of self-awareness, knowing both our strengths and our faults, in order to better ourselves in our work environment. You *can* make this happen on an individual basis. Take ownership in yourself, your company, your people, and your achievements, because no one will do this for you. Work with heart and purpose; frankly, there is no greater assembly of your talents to showcase than being authentic and displaying respect for yourself and others. Brands, whether big or small, will always leave impressions, but it is how you manage those impressions that will carve out your future.

You will always run into conflict and pitfalls; as the saying goes, "such is life." It is sometimes through these trials and tribulations that we become even stronger in our effort to build our personal brand. So, keep your perspective and take the time to step back from situations in order to evaluate strategically. The next move you choose will make a difference. I have yet to meet a client who has said, "My career path is easy." Why? Because it never is. But I assure you that using the many tools in this book will ease your way and accelerate your brand so that you do not feel as though you are constantly climbing the big hill.

What are you truly willing to do for yourself? What are you truly willing to do for others? Intention is a beautiful thing, but not acting on intention is staying complacent. Keep moving, keep learning, and keep growing, whatever that may look like for you.

Experience certainly comes in all shapes and sizes. After reading this book, if you need further coaching or guidance, feel free to reach out to my Peggy Noe Stevens & Associates image team at www.peggynoestevens. com. We will be happy to assist you! Professional presence is what we believe in, and we wish to share it.

ABOUT THE AUTHOR

For over twenty years, Peggy Noe Stevens has devoted herself to hospitality, entertaining, and the exploration of experiential marketing in both career and personal life. As a trained and certified protocol, image, and public speaking consultant, she uses a customized approach to establishing the authentic image architecture of both people and place. Because of her signature style, expertise, and creativity, she is retained by companies to seek out the true essence of image and identity. Her approach conveys powerfully targeted brand messaging through environments while building confidence, self-awareness, and professional presence in employees.

What she describes as the "architecture of image" (creating culture with style and substance) is a 360-degree approach to immersing the total self and environment in the image you wish to portray. Her experience has led her to develop strategic "culture marketing" for branded environments. This strategy also assimilates and aligns the individuals who work in those environments by masterfully constructing their personal brand. Her method takes a holistic approach to cultivating image and provides overall "image therapy" to her clients. The architecture of image begins with a complete and detailed assessment and leads to a blueprint transformation of your personnel, brand environment, or consumer experience.

She began her career in hospitality and marketing with Hyatt Hotels Corporation, engaging in all aspects of guest services, professional event planning, and the highest standards of culinary arts and entertaining. Peggy then moved to the Brown-Forman Corporation to lead a newly developed travel and event planning department. As global event planner, she managed more than one hundred events annually, negotiated multimillion-dollar travel contracts, and enhanced all aspects of travel, customer service, entertaining protocol, and hospitality for executives.

While at Brown-Forman, Peggy was also given the opportunity to move into the new frontier of experiential marketing, where she assimilated and directed an impressive portfolio of wine and spirit brand destinations and worked with such iconic brands as Jack Daniel's, Woodford Reserve Bourbon, Southern Comfort, Fetzer, and Sonoma-Cutrer Vineyards. In this role, Peggy's keen strategic direction and sense for establishing rich cultures positioned each destination to become a top attraction in its respective location. Directing all channels of destination management, she comprehensively fine-tuned experiential touchpoints with the consumer, from retail and aesthetics to culinary and tourism programs, creating one-of-a-kind, memorable experiences. She simply mastered the art of engaging people emotionally through the senses.

She particularly excelled at the overall crafting of the master plan by taking the origin of environments and their employees and determining the granular mapping of every aspect of image the brands wished to create. Peggy's career has allowed her to travel globally to observe the strengths and weaknesses of many brand cultures, and she is an expert in consumer-driven behavior as it relates to the brand and its environment.

In many ways, Peggy has been a trailblazer for women, and yet she has lived up to her heritage. She became the world's first female master bourbon taster and can trace her lineage back to some of the great bourbon-making families in Kentucky. She has been called the "Oprah of entertaining" and a "lifestyle maven." Also described as a "more relaxed Martha Stewart," she has represented Kentucky for such notables as Julia Child, Bobby Flay, and the prince of Spain.

Her executive leadership skills also enhanced her talent for designing women's strategy studies for corporations, and she has spoken to countless professional organizations about issues in the workplace and strategizing careers. She has set an inspiring new standard by which corporations can attract and retain female executives.

Mother, author, global speaker, media spokesperson, and prominent experiential brand strategist, Peggy brings a gracious, fresh, and relevant approach to establishing image. She engages audiences with her dynamic wit and energetic message.